If not You.....then Who?

Little questions about big things

Jan Storey

Published by Sakayi Publishing in 2012
Midwifed by Aileen Neilan
Copyright Jan Storey 2012
Jan Storey has asserted her right to be identified as author of this
work in accordance with the Copyright, Designs and Patents Act
1988.
Printed by Printers Empire
            8 Eskdale Grove
            Garforth
            Leeds
            LS25 2AU

1

Introduction
If not You...........then Who?

Hey you, the sleepwalker over there: time to wake up! Wake up and watch your usual, habitual self go through the motions day after day of your life towards your death. Why are you here? To mark time? To spend time? To waste time? To have a good time?

No, you are here to create something unique and graceful: something only you can do.

'But I'm busy', you say. 'I never have time to waste time. I have too much to do'. Much of what you do is disgraceful rather than graceful. You are unaware of yourself, of your motivations, your spirit or your great work, whatever that is.

You buy things, have things, get people, get cars, lose jobs, lose lovers, lose your reason for living and take up space with the stuff you accumulate.

What is your intention in being on earth at this time? What have you come here to do? Why are you here now? What will you do about the fact that you don't know?

Wake up sleepwalker. Your fear of failing has made you drowsy, dreamy; hardly here at all.

What is it you refuse to feel? Are you sure that numbing yourself into a trance is less painful than what you avoid. Why do you dumb down your beautiful self with TV, noise, meaningless relationships, busyness, cleverness, casual sex, drugs and alcohol?

Wake up dreamer. There is still some life left. Look closely at the stage, the scenery, the props, the costumes of the play that passes for your life. You created all that. You have proved you are a creator, so would you like to create something different now?

What can you do?

Make a start. Refuse to carry on being robotic. Change just one of your habits and the cause and effect of things will nudge you awake. Then you will be able to see the true significance of your everyday life.

You can cut the strings between you and the puppet masters that keep you numb, but you have to see those strings clearly first.

These pieces of writing, which I call Gracenotes, might help you along the way to seeing your strings more clearly. They are not intended to bring you to Wisdom, Truth or Enlightenment (whatever those words mean for you), but to poke you in the ribs and say, 'Oi you – wake up!'

Some of these Gracenotes may do that for you and some won't. If just one does, that's enough. Just one good 'Oi you!' will start the process of your waking. Once started, Grace will take care of the rest.

What I mean by Grace is...whatever in your experience has ever been beautiful, true for you and creates good in your life.

It doesn't matter in which order you read or where you start and finish. You may agree with some or none and disagree with many or all of them. That's fine. The process of coming to agreement or disagreement is useful in itself.

They may raise more questions than give answers. This is ideal as it wakes up the part of you that I call 'the inquirer'. The style of writing is bossy and declarative. I have included no sources or other contributors' ideas. Obviously, I have been affected and taught by others views, but they, like my own remarks are simply opinions and as such may have no substance in truth for you. It is for you to decide what your view is: that is the point and the outcome I hope for.

Each Gracenote represents a moment of waking in myself. My desire to awaken your awareness in this life has a hidden motive: I long for more awake lovers, awake friends, awake colleagues, children and neighbours.

'Why go to all this trouble?', you say. If you've ever made love to, worked or lived with someone who's asleep, or poured out your heart to someone who doesn't know how to listen, or longed for something you can't name to enliven your life, you will know why.

Jan Storey

1. What is Grace Anyway?

I sometimes think that Grace is much easier to see in its absence –
or at least it's easier to describe that way. Take the world we all live
in: it isn't hard to imagine scenes of war, the apparent riches of the
few and the visible starvation and lack of basics experienced by
those in developing countries. The pictures on television depict a
lack of Grace or often, even disgrace, in the way we treat ourselves,
each other and our planetary home, the earth.

When you are 'with or in Grace' you know it. When you witness it in
others you are aware that you are in the presence of something
extraordinary. For the Graced one, every sense is heightened, time
expands or collapses, there is no doubt that you can and will do
what you are attempting to do. Most curious of all, perhaps, is the
feeling that something enormously powerful is helping you to
achieve in that moment, exactly what you must.

Depending on your spiritual beliefs (or lack of them) you might think
of Grace in terms of the love of God, miracles ancient and modern,
magical occurrences, pie in the sky or the kindness of strangers.
Perhaps you consider Grace, if you consider it at all, as something
that you seldom witness or experience in your day to day life:
something belonging to another age and not about now at all.

These Gracenotes are an attempt to change your mind about that:
to make you more observant of, and more participative in, your own
daily life. Why would you want to bother to do that? After all, life is
effortful and time consuming just as it is.

It isn't quantity that I'm concerned with here (The amount of money
you have or don't have, the number of friends or lovers you have,
how much you get paid to do what you do or how many holidays a
year you take).

What I want to encourage you to do is to seriously consider the
quality of the life you lead, how satisfied you are with each moment
and what the point of each of your moments is.

It is more possible than you think to make your everyday life significant. Time isn't just for passing. It can be lived in and experienced fully.

* What do you believe you would have to give up to have a more Graceful life?

* How does Grace show itself in your life if it does? When do you feel most fulfilled; most at peace?

* Who is the most Graceful person you know? What are their most significant characteristics?

* Where and when do you feel the strongest sense of belonging?

There are no correct answers but consider quietly and see what insights do come.

Notes:

2. Are You Impatient?

What is it that creates the need for hurry and rush in you? Is it that you want to hurry towards your death? There's nothing wrong with that I guess, but it behoves you to live this life fully first.

How do you know that the speed you demand from yourself and from others is the speed that life should be lived at? The strange thing is that the more we hurry to cram more stuff into our lives, the less we live them. Why should this be?

Unless living has some spaces for thinking and reflecting in it, we just go around the same loop faster and faster. It is the spaces that are the learning time. The doing time between the spaces is where we test out what we reflected on and concluded from our learning.

No spaces means no learning. No learning means that you remain as ignorant as ever you were, and make the same mistakes in different ways over and over again.

Why are you so impatient with yourselves and with others? Your body knows the right speed to go. What makes you want to push it? I have heard you say, 'Oh, but I live a very busy life,', rather as if you are proud of it: as if that alone makes you something special. You were born as special as everyone else. Rushing through your life towards your death won't increase your specialness quotient – quite the reverse in fact.

What is it that's so scary in the spaces between doing that makes you afraid to pause and reflect? What might happen to you if you gave up your impatience and let it be?

How many things can you do well at any one time? Only one is the answer. So let that be the most important one, whatever that is for you. Do what matters most first, and do it very well. You waste time redoing the right things or doing the wrong things, when you rush and are impatient to get 'there' – wherever that is.

Value the spaces between the things you do. Value them much, much more than the things you do. In those spaces, that thinking and learning time, you gradually refine yourself and your life. You learn how to live and develop your intelligence. Slow down, pause, learn, change, realise.

* What are you rushing towards anyway?

* What will you do with the time you think you are saving?

* Pause deliberately every now and again. Breathe, see where you are and what you're really doing.

* Do one thing at a time and do it very well.

Notes:

3. What do you know about You?

If I asked you to tell me about yourself, what would you say first?

Perhaps you would tell me about what you do to earn money.
Maybe you would tell me whether you had a partner or children and
where you lived. These are things that you are doing or have done.
They aren't really telling me a lot about you are they?

What do you know about You? Could you describe what you are
feeling as you read these things? Do you know where in your body
you are feeling the things you feel?

What is the strongest belief you hold? Does that feel like a belief to
you or is it just an opinion? What is the difference for you? How
does that belief guide your life? If it doesn't, what does? Well
something must inform you and keep you on the straight and narrow
of your own values. What is it? What happens to you when you
leave the path of your own guidance? What does that feel like?

What is the one thing that you would never, ever do? Have you
thought about that recently? Are you sure that it is the 'one thing'?
Perhaps you have done the one thing you would never, ever do and
chosen another thing to take its place. What made you do that?

What are your deepest held values? Do you know or aren't you
sure? Sometimes we inherit our values from our parents and family
of origin. Sometimes that inheritance is taken on without much
forethought and sometimes the inheritance is rejected out of hand in
our adolescent years.

Our values become the cornerstones and 'guidelines' of our lives and
we use them automatically to decide what we will or won't, can or
can't do every day. If we aren't really aware of what they are, this
means that we may be running our lives to out of date rules, or
using values that are someone else's to make our decisions. In this
case, whose life are we living?

These guidelines are often behind the swift upsurge of negative feelings that occur when we think someone or something else has done something unpardonable. If we are using our values to make judgements about what is right and wrong in the world, perhaps it would be worth spending time to figure out what they really are and where they come from.

* Write down 10 of your most important values

* Are they yours or someone else's?

* Are they out of date: do they need updating in the light of your own experience?

* Can you think of a time recently where you have reacted negatively to a value that you no longer really believed in?

* Is there some putting right you need to do as a result of an over-reaction to a 'defunct' value or belief?

Notes:

4. What is your life made of?

It seems to me that our lives are made up of habits and creativity in proportions that differ for each of us.

The habit part of us operates when we do the things we do often, like going to work, eating, driving the car, having a shower etc. It's extremely useful to us as it avoids us thinking in depth about each of these everyday things every time we do them.

The problem is that if we aren't really alive, awake and present in the moment, the habitual part of our life can take over and we sleepwalk through our day even when we shouldn't.

How much of your time do you spend habitually?

The creative part of us is used when we meet something different, unexpected, shocking - or we imagine or create something new: something that didn't exist before.

When we are in that part of our lives we feel wide awake, lively and completely present to what is going on in every moment.

Living creatively sometimes takes us away from the shoulds and oughts of our lives. Once creativity overtakes us, more ordinary living seems very dull indeed.

Where and when do you live creatively and how much of your life is spent this way?

If most of your life is spent habitually you are sleepwalking. Continuous sleepwalking is a waste of the living life because you aren't really present – not really around to know what is happening inside or outside yourself.

Sometimes it happens that times in our lives seem full of repetitive activities. If this is the case for you, alter your habits a little. Go to bed at a different time, get up at a different time, eat something you would never eat, speak to strangers, have your hair cut differently, check out what you think you know is so, walk a different way to the shops or to work.   Don't be habitual: live a wide awake life.

* Keep a journal. Write down everything you do for a week that's habitual.

* Note when your mind becomes creative and you become alert and engaged in what you are doing.

* What wakes you up – dancing, running, making love, decorating the bathroom?

* What puts you to sleep – having sex, watching TV, driving?

* What percentage of your life is spent 'sleeping' (either real sleep or eyes-open sleep)?

• Is the balance between habits and creativity in your life right for you?

If not, what will you do about it? If not you, then who?

Notes:

5. What are your Saturdays like?

Is it tempting to think you know what Saturdays **should** be like? If so, it is probably also tempting to decide that your Saturdays are not like that even though other peoples' probably are.

Once you have decided that there is a big gap in satisfaction between your Saturdays and the gloriously enjoyable Saturdays experienced by others, then you can use your Saturdays to reflect deeply on what you don't have that other people do.

This way your Saturdays can be used for disappointment, envy and depression can't they. This gives a sort of legitimacy to them. Thank goodness for that. Your Saturdays are definitely for something, rather than nothing as you feared!
And guess what, you can apply the same process of 'less than-ness' to your:

Christmases
Birthdays
Relationships
Homes
Jobs
Bodies
Mondays, Tuesdays, Wednesdays, Thursdays, Fridays and Sundays.

How much of your life do you want to spend analysing, pondering and grieving for what you assume you don't have? Analysing 'the gap' will give you something to think about certainly. You will never have nothing to think about ever again.

Thinking regretfully about what you don't have will give your self a certain colour (grey) and flavour (bitter). It can make you and shape you and determine how others see you (self-pitying victim). It eats away at your energy and your willingness to take the initiative to change your circumstances for the better.

Perhaps it's time to look again. Look at what you do have for a change. Be grateful for what you have. Just for now, forget to long for what you don't have. See whether that doesn't improve your Saturday and everyone else's that you come into contact with.

* Saturdays are for cappuccinos and gratitude.

* Why is it so hard for you to say and mean 'thank you' for all that you have?

* What part does Gratitude play in Graceful living?

* What might you have to face up to if you lost your negative view of your life?

* What might you need to take responsibility for if you thought about what you had been given, rather than what you haven't been given by Life.

Notes:

6. Acknowledge what you can. Say 'no' to what you can't.

Sometimes we know we ought to speak up: we know we should say something but we stay silent; blurt out something terse or beat out a hasty retreat. This may be in response to an offer, a deal, a request, a question, an invitation or an observation that is unwelcome and unwanted.

Why do we make ourselves so awkward? Why don't we just say what we feel?

There are many reasons for this, but often it's because we feel two completely opposing things at once and aren't skilled at communicating both at the same time.

Suppose for instance someone you know makes you a kind offer that you are clear you don't want to accept.

This makes you feel awkward and what can you say?   You could mumble 'thanks very much,' and accept the unwanted offer (vowing silently never to take it up). You could say, 'there is absolutely no way I want that,' and avoid them thereafter.

Alternatively, you could try this:

Acknowledge the kindness of their intention:

'It's very kind of you to think of me.........'

But be firm in your refusal of what you don't want:

'.........but that isn't something I'd want to take you up on,'.

That way both truths (they thought of you) and (you don't want what is on offer) are honoured in the same sentence. When opposing truths are honoured in this way, your communication takes on a more Graceful style and your refusal is balanced with your respect for the humanness of the other individual. How what you say in this way is received by the other person is really up to them. You have done all you honestly can.

When we hear the truth, even though we may not like it, there is often a sense of completion that is eventually welcome.

* Acknowledge what you can

* Be firm and clear about what you can't

* Tell the truth about what you can no longer do, say or relate to

* How do you know when you have been told the truth? Where in your body do you acknowledge that something that you've heard is the truth?

What types of communication do you find most difficult to make and to whom. What should you be saying instead of avoiding and if not you, then who?

Notes:

7. Seeing the Grace in ordinary people and things

There is something Graceful in all living things. Living things have form and shape, body and structure, generative and degenerative processes.

Human beings have all those and more. We have the ability to deduce and reason, to have feelings and thoughts. Arguably we are free to make up our minds and to take action. We have choice. Our choices of action range from the basest and cruellest acts to the tenderest and most generous self sacrifice. We are capable of being less or more than human.

Many of us never realise this choice that either debases or elevates us in our humanness. One of the reasons for this is that we aren't sufficiently present in the present moment. Some sort of trigger happens in our lives and we re-act to it, often in a habitual or defensive way if we suppose the trigger to be dangerous or unpleasant.

Sometimes the re-action is to do with our past: something hurt us and we found a way to cope that worked; so we keep on doing it, possibly for the rest of our lives. Sometimes the re-action is to do with our future and threatens the idea we have of how we want that future to be; so we block it.

Either way, if you are able to meet that trigger completely in the present moment you would realise that there is no genuine threat to you now: the person that couldn't cope in the past has grown up somewhat and is much more resilient, and the person that you envisage in the future doesn't yet exist and therefore cannot be destroyed by what happens now.

The ability to stay grounded in the present when difficulty, loss or confusion arises, to wish neither to wound the other, nor to be wounded but to be entirely open and vulnerable nevertheless, is, I believe a Graced state or place of being.

When I am fortunate enough to witness someone acting from that undefended position, with all the uncertainty that brings, I can see Grace manifesting itself through human action.

* How easy is it for you to see vulnerability as a positive state to be in?

* What fears that you currently experience regularly in your life are based in the past and could be dispensed with now?

* What fears that spoil your enjoyment of life now, are really imaginings about the future that may never happen?

Notes:

8. Taking Offence is offensive!

People these days seem very quick to imagine themselves slighted.
When someone says or does something to us that we don't like, our
sense of dignity becomes affronted. We often take these things
personally. But let's examine this tendency a little more closely.

Imagine these scenarios:

* Just as you are about to reverse into a car parking space you had
been waiting for, someone else screeches up and parks before you.

* You are waiting in a queue to be served when someone jumps in
before you.

* You are practically pushed over by someone barging past you with
large parcels and shopping

* Someone in front of you lets the door swing shut in your face

* The motorist in front of you is going so slowly on a part of the
road where you just can't overtake and you are in a hurry.

These sorts of things and worse happen often. You feel your
emotions rise and you become affronted by what they have done or
are doing. The assumption is that they did it on purpose to you in
particular and it makes you angry. You feel like chasing after them
and putting them straight.

The mistake you make here is to believe that it is personally directed
at you, when in fact the other person has hardly noticed that you
exist. The mistake they make is one of unconsciousness, rather than
rudeness to you.

When you allow your ego to rule you, it seems as if most things that
happen in your world are intended either to please or displease you.
Why give yourself so much significance? Why give yourself so much
pain?

Look around you. You are one of many. Don't take so much offence, as this is, in itself, an offensive act. Don't take things so personally: they are really little to do with you.

* How much do you value your equanimity?

* How much do you value the ability to put people straight when they offend you?

* How many times a day do you catch yourself taking things personally and reacting?

* How many wars in our world have started because pompous people with inflated senses of their own dignity have decided that they have been offended and taken it personally?

Notes:

9. Sadness is for something

Such great store is set by being happy in our society. Whole industries are dedicated to making sure that we are all happy every day and every night. Looking at pictures in magazines of the young and beautiful enjoying themselves, you could feel guilty for not being ecstatically happy all the time.

But sadness is important too. First of all it balances our emotional swings. As with everything in nature, the highs need corresponding lows just as surely as night follows day. You are never taught how to be sad constructively are you? Don't you find that strange when there is so much emphasis on how to be happy effectively?

The character of sadness reminds us of the dark, rather than the light and solitariness rather than being in company with others. Again, darkness and solitariness are not states that we often think of as positive. Perhaps it's time to look again at this.

The dark night is a time of rest and recuperation. Our bodies recharge and we can enjoy some time asleep. For those who can't sleep it can be a creative time, a time where the imagination fashions stories, symbols and ideas that we can use to live our lives in a richer way.

Being alone is again something that our society doesn't appear to value. 'Successful' people are never seen by themselves are they? It might be worth considering the following:

Until you can be content in your own company, it will be difficult for you to be content in anyone else's.

A sad time is an excellent opportunity to bask in the creative darkness and to get to know yourself well. The feelings of lowness and slowness that come with sadness are definitely meant for something. Don't allow yourself to be distracted back into light happiness too quickly, or you will miss an opportunity for learning, growing and becoming more self-aware.

Don't miss your sad times – you need them.

* How do you avoid being sad?
* What distractions/addictions do you use to avoid your sad self?
* Try sitting alone in your home. What impulse or idea makes you jump up to 'do' something and how often? Who is pulling your strings at these moments?

Who's in charge of You. If not You, then Who?

Notes:

10. Where does Joy come from?

You may be walking along a street or going through your daily routine when suddenly, for no reason you can think of, you are Graced by a deep and sudden joy.

The feeling comes unbidden from inside: it isn't connected to anything outside yourself as far as you can tell. Everything in your world appears the same but somehow much more beautiful, much more important and full of meaning. You feel full of gratitude for the state you find yourself in.

Perhaps this feeling is the truth of your life: who you really are. Or perhaps you have slipped through the thin skin that separates your mundane world from this vibrant, joyful one.

Maybe you aren't simply a body, a brain and a mass of feelings? Being Graced by joy is an urging of the soul. Do you believe that? Are you sure? How can you know? (What do you think of when you read the word 'soul'?).

You might consider joy as a call to attend to the beautiful and the perfect in your life on this earth.

Everyday beauty and perfection is all around us in our partners, friends, homes, workplaces, streets, fields, woods, rivers and the great starry night sky. You don't believe me? Then what are you putting your attention on? You get what you dwell on. If you concentrate on ugliness and negative things, that is what you will notice in your life.

Forget modern criteria for what is beautiful. Decide on your own and look for beauty everywhere. Once you can appreciate what surrounds you in your people and your places, unbidden joy and deep gratitude for what you will be given completely free of charge will visit you more and more often.

How would that be for you? Good I think.

* Notice when you are visited by Joy – even if the visit feels fleeting

* Write down how things seem to you at these times. Read what you have written when you are feeling low and things seem bleak.

* What do you most dwell on? Is this really what you want in your life?

* What is the difference between being realistic and being negative for you?

* How do you express your gratitude and to who?

Notes:

11. Like fishes can't see water

Some things are so familiar, so all around us all the time that we
don't see them: until they aren't there any more that is. Then we
realise that we had them, haven't got them now and sometimes (but
not always) we miss them.

How is it that the things sweetest to us are initially held dear but
often gradually hardly noticed or taken for granted?

This can happen with lovers and partners. Initially we noticed
everything they did and said to us; every nuance, every mood, every
precious touch. All too often we eventually hardly notice they are
there most of the time and give what they say the most cursory
attention.

Think of the air you breath as a newborn: that first in-breath and
resulting pinking of the skin is a glorious sign of life. In later life we
hardly notice the process of breathing at all, until it becomes difficult
for some reason or another.

What about your home, your job or your car? When they were new,
you noticed every feature but time and unconsciousness takes the
edge off your observation and dulls your appreciation of what you
have.

What is this gradual lessening of appreciation and taking things for
granted about?

Treating things and people with deadening familiarity is another way
of being asleep. What is the point of being with dear ones and
collecting possessions if you no longer recognise them in the way
you did? This is often why people become serial partner swappers:
they no longer notice the one they have and need another one or an
add on to wake them up!

You can choose to do things differently. Stay awake. Don't become
familiar with the things and people you have in your life. Stay in the
present and treat everyone and everything you are with today as if

they are brand new to you. Notice what you once noticed. Say the things you used to say. Being awake in the present feels good, so..... choose to be that.

Turn the focus of your attention on what is important to you while you still have it.

* Think back to when you first met your partner or someone else dear to you. What did you notice about them then that you don't notice now?

* What would your life be like without the things and people that are now familiar to you?

* Breathe the blessed air and be grateful. Begin to notice when you breath in a shallow way persistently

* Do you think that fish see the water?

Notes:

12. Talk, Talk, Talk.

Do you recognise this?

'When you don't notice me when you talk to me and when you don't appear to see me, I lose my happiness and become sad at my core'.

'I had looked forward so much to seeing you. I had so many things to tell you. You told me about your day. You told me about how things were. You asked no questions about me'.

'I told you things. When I stopped talking you stayed silent for a second or two then said something else about you. What you said appeared to have no connection with what I said: no continuity'.

'What to make of this? What I say isn't interesting to you? There is nothing you can or wish to say about it? There is nothing you wish to know so you don't ask questions?'

Does that remind you of anyone? How does the process of a conversation become so unsatisfactory to one participant without the other appearing to notice or care? Perhaps it's because there are many different needs behind our desire to communicate with the ones we love:

* Simply to give or receive information

* To get an answer to what we say

* To have what we are saying **received** by someone else rather than being reacted to

* To hear our own voice out loud with an audience

* To listen and respond

* Through sharing thoughts to be fully seen and completely heard for whom we truly are

* Through conversation, to reconnect in a more intimate way with a loved one

Sadly, because two people may each have one of the above or some other reason for communicating, it's very common for each individual to be using the same conversation to satisfy an entirely different need.   At these times, neither person is likely to really get what they want. An unconscious talker will talk on regardless, but a speaker or listener who is awake will feel the pain or dissatisfaction from that.

Are you aware of the different needs behind your conversations with loved ones? Can you check it out within yourself and them?

Pay attention for the next few days. Discover why you talk and listen the way you do.

Do you notice when you switch off from important conversations? What do you do about it?

If you can't figure out why you are communicating, then stop babbling until you do.

Notes:

13. What does going deeper sexually mean?

Perhaps not quite what you think. If you are a sexually active person, what is sex for in your life?

When you make love you may think that you do it for yourself and your partner, which of course you do. But can something so potentially beautiful and meaningful be about just you and what you want?

Imagine: what if the sexual union of a man and a woman contained a power that fed the soul of the world?

If this were so, would you approach your partner differently?

The world's soul needs every act of complete and conscious union it can get. This need includes the coming together of nations in peace, the ability of families to live without conflict and the great religions of the world to build bridges and respect each other's differences.

Can you accept that this is so?

Would it be so far fetched to begin to consider your lovemaking as just as socially helpful as recycling things so that precious resource isn't wasted or making donations for those in need or planting trees to be enjoyed by future generations?

If conscious sex is indeed the model of perfect Universal union, how can you and your partner begin to acknowledge this responsibility and make love not only for yourselves, but for everyone?

* Stay wide awake when you make love, look into the eyes of your lover, see who they truly are and get a reflection back of yourself and what you are doing.

* At the moment of orgasm, lose your edges and become part of everyone and everything else. See this moment as a song of praise to life.

29

* Afterwards, don't hurry away from the expandedness you felt. You return to your small self soon enough. Try to take with you, into your everyday life; that sense of connection to everything else you experienced.

* Perhaps that way of considering sex is all too much to be credible for you. In any case, you can at least have fun investigating the notion of deeper sex for yourselves.

But perhaps the largeness of the merging is the truth of our existence. After all, it is possible that our individual and do-it-alone state is the real illusion.

Notes:

14. Living your life with rightness as a guiding principle

Is that what you think you do? Are you sure you know the difference between being a principled person to being a rigidly programmed know-all? Let's see if we can sort this out.

Sometimes living your life to what you consider to be sound moral values and principles is less ethical than you think. This sort of living is often based on the premise that there is but one set of 'sound moral values' that all beings should share, that this is the only right way to live and that you, personally are an expert at doing this!

Do you find yourself thinking or saying things like this:

'Things should be done this way and not that way. (Why can't you see that?)'.
'I believe in this and not that. (And you should too).
'You must be able to see what to do in this situation? (There is, after all, only one thing that can be done and that is the thing I think is right).
'Surely all good/sane/principled people can see that this is the only right course of action! (Because I can see clearly, I am good/sane/principled and as you can't see, you obviously aren't but I will put you straight!).
'We all know/believe in doing it this way don't we? (You are too weak or stupid to take the proper course of action so I will shame you into it).

The above may make you smile. Perhaps you recognise yourself, or refuse to recognise yourself in these statements. You may live or work or otherwise be on the receiving end of words like these. But what is it that makes some of us communicate and think in this way?

Perhaps we had the idea of wrongness brought very forcibly to our attention when we were too young to do anything other than feel very ashamed of not getting it right or ever being right in our own selves. To help us cope with this heartbreak, which we accepted as truth, we determined never to get it wrong if we could help it. We decided for ourselves what rightness looked like and stuck rigidly to it as a survival strategy for life. We believed we had detected that if we wanted to be loved and valued we had to be right, get it right, know what was right – and never be wrong (or if we were, never, never to admit to it).

Does this have an echo of the truth for you? What can you do for yourself or encourage a loved one to try, if rightness is coming between you in a problematic way?

* Be tender with the need to be right and see it for what it is – a lifelong fear of getting things wrong and not being valued or loved because of that. Appreciate your own struggle and allow yourself to wear the label 'courageous' instead of 'right'.

* Listen more to others' views. Notice the differences and the variety of opinion. Consider those most different from your own for their merits and originality. Learn to love the energy of ideas and to play with them, even if they are difficult to accept.

* Practice conceding with Grace to someone else's view

Notes:

15. Do you have the capacity to be affected?

To what extent do you allow yourself to be deeply affected or moved by your life? Do you try to limit or numb yourself in order not to feel? There are many ways available to do this; alcohol, tobacco, drugs, television, persistent noise etc.

Why do you do this? Are you afraid you will be overwhelmed by what you feel?

Each of the ways of numbing or deadening carry a price. Perhaps one of the least considered are certain types of television, DVD or film that are common at the moment. Today we are assaulted with so many moving images: people and other living beings in the throes of extreme life and death experiences which once would have shocked us to the core.

As if these aren't graphic enough, animations, which become more and more sophisticated technically and lifelike, depict all manner of terrifying and horrific images. These are available in the form of video games to be bought by adults and children alike.

Human beings were designed with an inbuilt process of shock that normally operates when someone sees or experiences something too terrible for them to deal with. Once upon a time watching people being torn limb from limb would have been included in that category. But now people are actually choosing to witness scenes like this for entertainment!

What will the effect of this be on our species in the long term?

In the medium term the sensitivity that once would have affected us deeply when we were subjected to horrifying images is being deadened.

What have you become used to that once would have horrified you?

Have you become bigger, tougher, stronger, rougher as a result of this change? Have you been coarsened and desensitised too?
If you removed your ability to be affected by a process of constant exposure to horror, how much of your human sensitivity would you sacrifice also?

What will you do when you need to be sensitive, loving, tender and vulnerable if you can no longer access these feelings? Will you just become tough instead?

* Identify the feeling in your body when you watch a particularly brutal scene on television or at the cinema? Can you name that feeling?

* How would you describe your capacity to be tender? Check your answer with your partner or a friend.

Notes:

16. How can you live a bigger life?

Do you ever experience a sense of smallness; a feeling that as far as life is concerned you are hardly here at all?

Do you sometimes slip between people in crowds and have a sense of passing almost unseen in the streets, shops and at work?

Who is it that is seeing itself as small?

What is the nature of the one who believes itself to be insignificant?

Some people believe it is right to have a clear idea of their own unimportance. They see it as 'knowing their place'. Along with this idea often goes a sense of lack and a mindset that anticipates no improvement or increase in their ability to get any of their needs met.

There is an arrogance in not expecting much and making your own life unimportant and small. What's so special about you that you don't remain open to the largesse of life and the world in which you live? Why consider yourself so especially deprived?

No matter what your physical and financial circumstances may be, you are completely free to choose what you feel about them.

Perhaps you don't feel you have any particular talent and gift to Grace your life and the lives of others. Some folk are gifted with an extraordinary power to be ordinary and everyday. If this is you, grow into it and make your ordinariness superb.

If you think of yourself as plain or unattractive compared to others, stop this now. Comparisons like this are useless because you aren't measuring like with like. There is no-one exactly like you and you could make the most of that or complain. The choice is absolutely yours. Will you feel happy or miserable? Will you make yourself small and insignificant or expand to fit the space life provides you with?

This is nothing to do with speaking more or louder, taking up more physical space, having your view known more widely or dressing in a showier way. This is to do with how you decide to think about yourself and your life.

Have the Grace to see your own uniqueness and live gently from that surprised and expansive place.

* When did you decide how you were going to feel about yourself today?

* Try making the decision before you get up. Spend a few moments awake and being grateful to find yourself in this body, in this life.

* Don't let other people decide how you should be feeling about yourself. Don't change your mood as a reaction to to others' carelessness of you or any putdowns you might receive.

Starting from this moment, today, choose to live bigger from the inside and let the outside take care of itself.

Notes:

17. How do you make tea?

Do you ever worry about the state of your mind? Is it here, there and everywhere? Are you thinking of a thousand things at once and none of those very well?

Sometimes it helps to practice letting your mind rest on one thing at a time. This grounds and centres us. It also brings a deep appreciation for very familiar things.

Take one thing that you do every day, do it slowly and let your mind rest on your actions as you do it. Try this as you make your next cup of tea:

* Take the kettle to the tap (or the water filter) and watch the water sparkle into it. What processes have had to happen for the drinking water to get to you? Think about the brilliant ideas and the efforts of those who first designed and built water filtration systems and the pipe work that brings it to your home.

* Turn the kettle on or place it on the lit hob. Do you take your gas or electricity for granted? Appreciate the heat generated and all the things you are able to do because you have it.

* Pour the boiling water into the pot (or the cup). Notice the pattern or glaze on your china or pottery and any pattern on it that you have ceased to notice through familiarity. Is it smooth or grainy to the touch.

*Fetch the milk if you take it. Is it delivered daily to your door or do you fetch it from the supermarket or shop? Either way, consider the process of milking the cow, once done by hand and now usually by machine and what happens to the milk to make it safe to drink.

* Pour the tea into the cup. As the steam rises notice the aroma of the leaves or tea bag. Be aware of the golden colour in the light. How many human beings were involved in planting, picking, and processing the leaves in countries far away. What are their lives like compared to yours?

* Take your tea and sit with it: the cup or mug between your hands and notice the comfort of the familiar moment. How many others, in so many different circumstances, are doing this same small ritual right now? Wish them all peace.

* Sip the liquid and as you feel it go down inside you imagine the warm glow produced by so much human activity and effort spread and comfort you. Remember yourself as part of this web of humanness and enjoy the feeling of belonging.

* If there is time, sit quietly for a few minutes. Appreciate the small ritual you have just undertaken, in very ordinary circumstances. Try to do something similar every day to still and then focus your mind and to practice gratitude for the ordinary things that make up your life.

Notes:

18. Are you sentimental?

Sometimes we feel so much, so often and for so many that our whole being begins to operate from a soggy mush of sentimental feeling. Emotionally, we start to function unintelligently

Where real feeling has been coarsened by subjecting it to too much horror, genuine compassion and tender feelings are often expressed, almost in contrast, via the sickly sweetness of sentimentality.

Look around you at advertisements in magazines and newspaper articles. If we are not reading about massacre and murder, we are looking at illustrations of puppies, Christmas snow scenes and nice family scenarios around the Sunday lunch table.

Most of the truth and reality of our lives is somewhere between the horrific and the sentimentally sweet. The ability to feel and express compassionately and appropriately to what confronts us is becoming a rare 'skill'.

Compassion is a response of the heart and mind. It often has a component of action attached to it, but not always.

The difference between sentimental sympathy and an empathic, compassionate response to another's trouble, is the amount of imagination we add to what we are seeing in their 'story'.

If we are beginning to imagine what it would be like for ourselves if their 'story' happened to us, then we will begin to feel the emotion we would feel in that situation too. Our concern for them has slipped sideways into concern for us. The resulting mix of feeling is expressed as a sentimental, sympathetic response which isn't helpful.

Perhaps you consider yourself to be a kind and caring person and perhaps you are. But check out whether your communications are often sympathetic and sentimental.

If most of them are, ask yourself what need of your own you are attempting to satisfy by 'getting off' on another's sad story. Are you addicted to joint moaning? Are you trying to prove a theory that we all lead sad lives?

* Try acknowledging another's difficulty without including your feelings of what it would be like if it happened to you into the mix.

* Figure out for yourself the difference between compassion and sentimentality and notice how you might gravitate between one or other in your responses.

* Notice where you turn towards sentimentality in an attempt to get your need for tenderness met. (A little sentimentality is ok, but a lot will turn you to slush!)

* How exactly does tea and sympathy feed you? What is it you are really wanting?

Figure it out and ask for it straight.

Notes:

19. Is there Grace in surrender?

Today winning is something that we all want to do and losing or failing is what we most hope to avoid. Maybe you are good at winning; at being better than others or generally getting the last word or getting the last seat on the bus.

This allows you to think of yourself in a certain positive way and that your place in the family of things is secure. Even quite young children at school quickly pick up a sense of where they are in the class order in terms of achievement.

It might be interesting for you to try assuming that your place in the order of things is secure whether you win or lose in the game of life.

Surrendering brings up pictures of losers in battle, creeping toward the victor waving a white flag, with all the connotations of shame and failure that might bring.

There is a different type of surrender that has strength and nobility in it. This involves surrendering the ego, conceding a point, allowing another to walk through a door before you, letting go of the opinion you were so keen to impose, asking what you have done to make another unhappy and how you can put things right, serving someone else's interest before your own.

What is the strength and power in giving way in this manner? In the letting go of the desire to win or get one over on someone else, we realise that it didn't matter anyway and we feel an ease or peace within ourselves about our own behaviour.

Trying to be better than others takes up so much of our energy and is very different and less interesting than being the best we can be. So how will we know the difference between beating someone else and being our best selves in life.

The best we can be or the best we can do each moment is reaching forward to fill the space that life provides us with. The urge to do this is a non-competitive drive stretching us towards our potential.

It is never petty enough to want to get one over on someone else or subdue someone else in argument: never small enough to gloat at feeling overdog to someone else's underdog.

* When did you last 'subdue' your partner or a friend in an argument? What happened subsequently?

* How could you surrender your desire to be better than others? Who or what could you surrender that to?

* Can you see yourself as an equal in 'the place of things'? If you can't, what would you need to surrender before this would be possible?

* How attached are you to your role at home or at work? Does holding onto this role involve you in constantly fighting to keep it? What would it be like to surrender?

However, if you always find yourself giving way in your life and consequently, letting go of your dearest dreams, bring to mind what you most believe in and start living that.

Notes:

20. Do you have a daily practice?

Writing these 'if not yous' is one of mine. This is a time when an idea I have is brought out of my head and onto paper. It's a way to share with others something I hope may be helpful.

It has become a helpful habit to me. Something I do first thing after getting up and making tea. It anchors and starts my day.

While I write I become very peaceful and grateful for this time to be creative. Sometimes the words just flow through me and become an instruction to write this or that. At other times, it's harder work and nothing comes so easily. At these times my perseverance is tested and I congratulate myself when at last I finish.

Often morning times can be very busy, particularly when you are rushing off to work or getting children to school. So choose another time for your daily practice.

The most important thing is that your practice is mindful; that your world slows down and you bring to mind who you are, what you have and acknowledge it thankfully. If you have time to light a candle, its soft light will help to focus and calm you.

Sitting with a candle works very well at the end of the day too. Be mindful of your breath as it rises and falls. Breath out those things in your day that have hurt or angered you; don't take them to bed with you.

Think of one thing that you are proud of or has pleased you. Have the Grace to say thank you to the Source of All things, whatever or whoever you believe this to be.

If you are disappointed or worried, ask to see a way through or to know what to do. Be willing to listen for an answer. Keep it simple. Just sit mindfully for a while and do it every day.

* What are the reasons you are finding now for not being able to do this?

* Can you think of a place for your practice: in bed before you get up, in the train or bus, in the park, in the kitchen or in bed before you go to sleep?

* How many times do you think you would have to do your practice before it becomes a little ritual that you are pleased to do every day?

* Ideally a private place is best but practically this may not be possible. As your practice is based on being in a mindful state, it can happen almost anywhere.

* Try it. It will sooth and refresh you and you will soon look forward to it.

Notes:

21. Do you long for World Peace?

For those of us that believe in peace, it is easy to lose hope for the world. Sometimes the amount of violence, hatred and cruelty seems overwhelming.

It often appears that there is nothing that an ordinary person can do to make any difference and we feel completely disempowered in the face of how things are. For some people, the despair they feel leaks into the rest of their lives, making things seem frightening and the future bleak.

That is sometimes a good time to examine ourselves to see how much peace lives inside **us** and how much peace we bring to our daily situations. It is fruitless to look out there for the cause of aggression in the world, until we take responsibility for ourselves.

You may argue that giving someone a black look or shoving back because they trod on your toe in a crowd, is a very different order of things to mass murder somewhere else on the globe. Indeed the order is different, but the category of behaviour is much the same in that there is no good will or peaceful intent in either.

If every human being had only good will and peaceful intentions inside him or her, then atrocities couldn't happen.   It is as simple as that and therein lies some hope.

It makes sense then, if you care, to begin with you. Check out how many times a day you wish something less than positive for another.

If you aren't satisfied with what you find, begin to do something about it. Just suppose that every war had as its very first vibration someone giving another a black look. The escalation of that bad vibration through human behaviour could eventually become some sort of violent incident in the world.

Don't let the vibration begin in you.

* What sort of behaviour in others pulls you from your centre into a state of ill will?

* Why do you think it does this? What does it remind you of?

* When you feel your intention towards another become less than peaceful, what can you do about it?

* Notice how one person in a bad mood can affect everyone else in the room. See how this can escalate.

* When you are sitting quietly, check out the sense of peace within you. Imagine this peaceful energy radiating out into your home, your town, your country.

* Take responsibility for world peace. There is something you can do – let it start in you.   If not you, then who?

Notes:

22. What are you hiding?

There is something hidden in what you are. Under what you chose to show – what you put out there as your public face which helps you choose what you want people to think about you – there is something infinitely Graceful and much more precious .

There is something inside us. Perhaps it is the seed of what we are destined to become, that may or may not ever be seen or come to fruition in this life.

You can see this sometimes in others in the eyes of a very young child or perhaps an elderly person. Something from deep down, far away looks back at you and when you look again to check it out, it's gone.

It's as if you meet that other person's spirit or essence and it knows yours: a real homecoming and recognition.

So what is it that looks out of your eyes eager to meet the other?

It is something true and wise that knows what it's looking for and why?

Why isn't it like that for people all the time? Who really knows? Maybe we are too busy and too scared that something else might see beneath what we hope we seem like to others.

What do you hope you seem like to others?

What are you afraid will be seen and want to hide?

Where is the hidden one hiding in you?

How can you find out more about it?

Be still and catch yourself unawares when you aren't pretending. The hidden you is a shy creature that will show itself if you're patient.

You might also need to stop believing that you know how you (and anyone else for that matter) should be.

Be a true inquirer into who and what you are. Begin to greet your true self, the hidden one, with gentleness and acceptance.

Who knows what you will discover?

Notes:

23. How much time do you spend fixing things?

Do you think ahead and manage things carefully? Do you do this in order to make sure that bad things don't happen between you and others? Perhaps you do this because you believe that life should be nice and smooth for you and the people you know or love.

So what's wrong with doing that sort of 'fixing' all the time? Well, think what you could do with all the energy you spend being anxious enough to fix things so that nothing goes wrong. Life could unfold in the way it wanted to instead of being arranged and controlled by you.

What would you be like if you didn't feel responsible for keeping things from going wrong? What would people see if they saw you not fixing things? What would they see you doing and hear you saying if you weren't so anxious?

What does it feel like to be unafraid that something will go wrong? What would your body look and feel like if it weren't afraid? How would it be for your body if the life living in it weren't afraid of the truth between it and others?

If there were no fear of the truth between you and others what would it be like? Perhaps you could enjoy more Graceful relationships with other people.

What could you be saying and doing differently to enable this to happen?

If others could show you that they weren't afraid of your answers and you could be unafraid of their questions, what would you say to them?

* What is the worst thing that could happen anyway?

* Is there really anything worse than spending life fixing things instead of just spending life living?

* Think about it: there is nothing more terrifying than your own worst fantasy of what others think about you. What they think isn't your business anyway.

* Stop fixing and controlling and find out what's real.

Notes:

24. If only ......

If only your life wasn't so difficult. If only there weren't quite so many things stacked up against you being happy. If only everything was less problematic!

If only there weren't so many reasons 'why not'.

Did you get up this morning feeling glad to be alive, or did you drag yourself from your bed feeling heavy and weighed down? If I asked you what was preventing you from being happy would you tell me something like this:

* ...if only I could find somewhere else to live...

* ...but I can't do that because I don't have enough money...

* ...can't get a better job to earn more because I live too far from the city...

*...won't move into the city until I get a better job...

...and on and on.   In this sort of scenario we build up a huge sticky net of reasons why we can't do what we say we want to do. Our response to any offer or helpful suggestion tends to be, 'I could, yes, but...'. All we can produce are reasons 'why not'.

We give the fact that we are suffering from so many different difficulties and problems in our lives as the reason we can't begin to shift them. We are weighed down under the burden of layers of difficulty and can't see where to make a start to improve things. So we do nothing except moan about it.

Our belief that we have many problems is a mistake. We have only one. The one we have is an important one that affects everything we will ever do in our lives to change things for the better. The one problem we have is that we will not give up our fear in order to put an end to our suffering.

What is the nature of this fear we won't give up?

* we are fearful because we don't know what will happen if we stop being afraid

* we are afraid because we may hurt others or gain their disapproval if we stop being scared and make the changes we say we want

* we are frightened of how expanded and new our lives might become if we lose our fear and move forward

So we hold on to all our problems tightly because in their way they are a defence against fearless living. We continue to suffer because we are afraid to surrender to our fear and just step forward into the freedom of truly living.

How long will you continue to make your excuses? How many times will you say 'yes but', to the world. When will you surrender and say, 'Yes Please'? If now now, then when?

Notes:

25. Are you good at celebrating?

I don't mean be a first rate party person. This is usually what we first think of when we hear celebration mentioned.

Party-type celebration is the external manifestation of gratitude shared with others. There may be food and drink, music and dancing. It is usually because something good has happened: a 21st birthday, a wedding, the end of something difficult, someone's football team has won the cup or because it's Friday night.

These can be really uplifting occasions, but you don't have to wait for a public occasion to celebrate. Personal celebration of the things you have to be grateful for in your life can and should happen every day.

How might you do this?

* Take a big lungful of the air you get for free, smile and think 'thank you'. You can do this anywhere you find yourself to be

* Consider a friend, whether they are with you or not right now. Think about the extra pleasure you have in your life because of them. Hold them in your mind for a moment and think, 'bless you'.

* Flush the loo! Thank goodness human beings were clever enough to design modern sanitation systems.

* Slow down and really taste your food. Be truly grateful for the earth that provided it, the supermarket who sold it to you and the cook.

These small, personal celebrations change the nature of your day if they become a part of what you do regularly. Why is this?

Celebrating often, rather than moaning often, gives you a Graceful heart. A Graceful heart is grateful and by this means changes your energy and affects you and the people around you. When this happens, you attract positive people and events towards you. There is something quite irresistible about grateful energy in another.

This type of approach to life – a celebratory approach – increases your own sense of well-being and joy. This in turn positively affects the health of your body and mind.

The next time you wake up heavy and weighed down with trouble and worry, pause in your thinking and ask yourself what there is about your difficult situation that is good for you. Perhaps your car has broken down and you have to catch the bus, your lover has left you feeling very alone, your child is sick or you don't have enough money to pay your bills. These are all difficult things, but somewhere you will be being given the opportunity to do things, or think of things differently.

What opportunities are presenting themselves to you through your trouble? Everything you have to face promotes your growth.   Now that is something to celebrate.

Perhaps you are being given the opportunity to stop taking certain things for granted, to use your initiative, to show that despite all, you still have faith that life in all its Grace will support you. Celebrate that fully and notice the difference in your ability to cope with what you are presented with in life and to do something about it.

Celebrate you! You are a Graceful wonder.

Notes:

26. How privileged are you?

What does privilege mean? The dictionary describes it as a benefit, favour or advantage enjoyed only under special conditions. So are you aware of feeling privileged?

Some people are wealthy and enjoy the privileges that brings. Others have extraordinary beauty or intellect. Some live in amazingly scenic places. There are many other ways that human beings are considered privileged.

Perhaps as you read this you can't immediately think of anything that comes under the 'privileged' category for you. You can't bring to mind any particular benefit, no-one seems to want to do you too many favours and you are inclined to consider yourself as disadvantaged rather than see too many advantages in the way you live.

Perhaps the biggest privilege that any of us are granted, is life.

We are given this time, this life, and we are given free will to use it. We may not all be given the same length of life, but while we have it, we are endowed in the most precious of all ways.

Not really being conscious of the gift of Grace that life is, is a bit like buying something beautiful to wear and never finding a special enough occasion to wear it or having a gleaming sports car and always keeping it in the garage waiting for a day without rain.

Every day is special enough to let your life be significant.

It may be Monday morning, it may be raining, you may be out of a job or overdrawn at the bank, but it's still a special occasion that you could use to be mindful of the amazing privilege of living your life.

* Are you keeping your life for 'best'?

* Are you waiting for a special occasion some time in the future to bring it out?

* How do you know you will still have it?

* What are you waiting for?

You have been selected to live the life you have. It was never intended for anyone else but you and if not You, then Who?

Don't waste time. Move through your day being completely aware of the boundless privilege that you have been granted: your Life.

Notes:

27. Tell me how I am – but do it my way!!

There is a common thought process, perhaps just out of our awareness, that goes a bit like this:

' I really have nothing to say – nothing worth saying. But I keep on trying – trying to say something worthwhile. What is this need to say, speak, communicate, that humans seem to have? Why don't I just keep quiet?

What's in it for me to do this?

If I speak to you, I can tell you what I think: what I think about you, what I would like you to think about me, what I want to do, what I want you to do, what I want you not to do (to me).

Why do I need you to know how I feel about these things? Why is it not enough just to be clear about these myself? Why, sometimes, am I not able to be clear about these things myself and hope I will become clearer when I have spoken and you have replied?

Sometimes I define myself by what you say to me. Sometimes I don't like what you say about me Sometimes you are 'wrong' in what you say. Sometimes I may punish you by disliking you when you are 'wrong' about me. Sometimes I may tell you what I'm feeling and sometimes I won't. Why?

Why do I invest so much in your positive views about me, spoken through your words uttered with such magic, accuracy and rightness and then discount your words utterly when I don't agree with what you say?

Are you really a separate person when agreeing with me from the you who doesn't? If not, why do I treat you so differently?

Sometimes you are so gifted, so clever, so sensitive in what you say about me (when I agree with what you say). Why do I put the burden of defining me onto you in this way? Perhaps it's because I can't be bothered to know myself and hope you will do this for me.

I never ask your permission for this. I just hope – but I don't usually know I am hoping until you get it 'wrong' about me and then I am angry and disappointed.'

Reading the above you might believe that you never ask anyone to define you in the way I've described.

Perhaps....but then why do you take it all so personally and feel so hurt and angry about what people sometimes say that is 'wrong' about you?

* Why invest precious energy in other people's opinions (whether they are positive or negative about you) as though they were The Truth and not just opinions?

* Why waste time making yourself unhappy when others don't say or think what you want them to about you?

* Think about it: notice what you say and do. What is an opinion and what is the truth for and about you?

Do you only want to spend time with people who are 'right' about you and agree with you?

What would you miss out on if you did this? How bored would you like to be?

Notes:

28. Who or what do you serve?

We rise in the morning, do what we do all day and go to sleep at night. At the very least that is a pattern of an ordinary day and one that many people will recognise.

Sometimes a human being might stop and think or rebel against the feeling of being on a meaningless treadmill with the cry, 'There has to be more than this.' But what more should there be? What can we do to bring specific meaning and purpose into the habitual round of daily life?

The question, 'Why am I doing this?' or 'What am I doing this for?', can be useful. For some of us, the answer might be 'To survive', but this in itself can be a habit: the notion that we won't survive if we don't keep on keeping on. Most of us in the western world are actually much more than just surviving, even if we aren't finding much to inspire us in our nights and days.

When inspiration is lacking, life can seem very empty and without purpose. We look outside ourselves to others to inspire us – and they may – but not in a lasting way if when we look inside we find only self-serving ideals and motives.

Human beings are curiously split. We have learnt through the ages to become more and more interested in what we want and what we have and haven't got. By contrast, we also have a drive to use ourselves to serve something greater than we can individually be. Sometimes these two longings operating side by side can cause a lot of confusion for us and we swing between them in an erratic way.

To fully grow and be whole, a person needs to know that they are in the service of a superior Law. This may be a belief in compassion, the worship of the Source of all things, an idea in the freedom of all living beings, the notion of the relief of suffering for living beings, etc.. But the idea alone won't serve: true service needs the component of action added to the belief or idea to make it work in the world.

So what is it that you are here to serve? Which graceful and superior Law will guide you in return for your duty or devotion?

Be assured that a lifelong devotion to 'ME' will eventually bring with it a kind of apathetic despair and a feeling of leading an empty life, no matter what has been accomplished in the material sense. The getting up, doing what you do, going to bed sort of life is the result of not being in touch with a greater purpose; not serving something with Grace.

The emptiness can be changed quite easily if you remain very present as you go through your day mindful of what you are doing and why. If you are caring for your family do it without begrudging and realise then that what you are serving is Love.

If you work in a teaching capacity, have patience and kindness for people who are slow to learn or disruptive. They are fearful and you will have to serve that fear with Compassion even though others' behaviour sometimes makes it difficult for you recognise this.

If you are shopping, take time to acknowledge the person serving you as a human being and not a machine. Every interaction is an opportunity to serve a better way of communicating with each other.

If you continue along this path of everyday service, you will soon realise exactly what it is you are here to serve. A pattern or preference for being with others in a certain way will become apparent to you. Your perseverance will be rewarded with the certainty of what you are in service to and the purpose of your life will begin to become clear to you.

Notes:

29.   Doubting Thomas.....bye, bye.

Are you a 'doubting Thomas? Are you a sceptic? It **is** wise to be cautious isn't it? There are so many people out there trying to 'get you' aren't there?

How do you know this? You read the newspapers: watch the news on television. 'Unscrupulous people are everywhere,' you say, so you are justified in your doubt and your caution.

Let's examine the case you are making for doubt. Think carefully of the possible cost of 'coming unstuck', being 'taken for a ride', becoming the victim of a liar, a fraudster, a conman or woman. I see the basis of your argument.

But there is another way to consider the debate and it goes like this: what is the true cost of keeping yourself, your belongings and concerns confined, locked away, stored in safekeeping? If you doubt your ability to be safe enough in the world, how can you live fully in it?

You have a point because yes, sometimes bad things do happen to good people. But think carefully: what happens to doubting, sceptical, stay-at-home or lock-it-all-away and keep-it-safe people?

Nothing happens and how interesting is that?

And what happens to don't-let-anyone-in, don't-let-yourself-out people.

Nothing and no-one happens. Nothing comes in and nothing goes out and how isolating and lonely is that?

The true cost of a defending-against, protecting-from and doubting life is a small, tight, self constructed prison of scepticism and doubt. What can this lead to but a virtual, unlived life.

Are you too doubting of life to live it in a bigger way? Is your small cell enough for you? What a painful way to guard yourself from things that may never happen anyway, and in the event that they do, you might learn from, recover and move on.

How long will you keep this up? Until your life ends and your doubting with it? If your answer is **NO** to a life lived doubtfully, when and how will you swap this for something new – today, tomorrow, next year? If not now, then when?

You can change it in an instant. Allow your thinking to expand and follow these steps if you wish to be free:

1. Realise that your doubt isn't a reason not to live life and do things, but is an indication of **why** you don't want to take part: it is simply information about the nature of your fear. It is teaching you about yourself. Inasmuch as it remains only this it is really useful.

2. But understand that if you don't take part in living because of your doubt, you won't be able to take part in your own life's direction and growth: something/someone else will do that for or to you.

3. See it as gardeners do. Anything living that is not growing is probably dying. Make your choice now.

4. Accept that everything you are trying to keep safe and protect (whether it is your heart, your home, your car, your reputation or those you love), will one day have to be left behind when you leave life.

5. Therefore, make a decision about whether to continue to put all that doubting, defending energy into protecting what you have, or whether to stop now while you have free choice.

Is it really worth the risk of never taking a risk?

Even in the worst case you may find that losing things and people, although painful at the time, opens you to a more courageous life full of greater possibility.

Be prepared to love it and/or lose it (whatever it is) without doubting and protecting. Then you may not have to.

So say it now and mean it: 'bye, bye Doubting Thomas'. If this is not you, then who?

Notes:

30. Do you wake up feeling down?

Why is it that you get up feeling heavy, tired or sad in the mornings? (If you do). You can waste quite a lot of time trying to figure out why.

Who knows what our energetic selves do in the night; what dreams or night journeys you have been on; what quests or wanderings you have been involved in.

Treat the body kindly. Wash it gently and dress it with care. Welcome yourself back to the day. If there is time, sit for a few minutes with a lit candle. Ask that you are fully returned to yourself to begin your day and begin to look forward to it.

We are often unkind to ourselves, hating the way we feel. We sometimes dislike the way our body looks and expect it to work well and feel good for us. Do you work well for someone who dislikes you?

Open the window and breathe deeply. Filling your morning self with breath is not just about getting air into the lungs. The breath fills you with life force and you breathe out any staleness you feel to become regenerated.

Set yourself an emotional errand for the day. It could be something like this:

* to smile at people you meet

* to pay attention to what you feel but not necessarily to react to those feelings

* to totally accept how you look and feel

* to spend a few minutes 'seeing' the air you breathe moving around the body like light

* to remain centred no matter what goes on around you

Mornings are for setting your face towards yourself again. We turn away from ourselves and dislike so much about us so often that it's not surprising that we rise without looking forward to a new day.

How you feel at the beginning of a new day is really up to you. If you were your own lover, how would you treat you? What would you do and say to make that lover feel loved and ready to face a new day?.

Perhaps it's time you started to love yourself a little more then you could get up feeling up instead of down.

Notes:

31. Do you experience famine and feast in your life?

People often say that certain things in life are like buses: they all come along together and then there's a big gap!

I suppose they are referring to the strange ebb and flow of things that means that sometimes there are good things happening (or appearing to be), and then there is an arid time with none (or so it seems).

We tend to see this ebb and flow as a negative thing, particularly as it often seems as though the times of 'famine' are far longer than the times of 'feast'. We never seem to be prepared for the times of non-happening, even though this may be part of a familiar story in our lives.

Why are we not prepared when this is the way it has always been?

The seasons ebb and flow with life and then apparent death, night follows day, boiling water condenses into steam which becomes water again when it lands on a cool surface, people die, babies are born, the weather is warm then cools, birds migrate then return.

Everything sentient seems to cope with cycles of plenty and scarcity except human beings. But why is this? It is hard to know for sure, but we can guess that it might be something to do with our inability to appreciate 'down time'; that gap between one thing and another thing in our lives.

Perhaps we don't see 'down time' as a thing in itself; some thing or some time to be used for a purpose. We prefer to get it over with as quickly as possible and get to the next happening in our lives with the minimum of delay.

We don't allow ourselves to lie fallow. We call this doing nothing.

Some of us calculate ways to avoid down time by becoming busy with trivia. Think of the chaotic effect on nature if trees and plants did that. We cram our activities so closely together that one thing runs into another. Doing this takes the Grace from the rhythms of life and postpones important reflecting time for another time: usually never.

It also means that you aren't giving important parts of your life to your dear ones, because you are using people simply to fill the silent spaces in your existence. Do they know that? Have they agreed to being used by you in this way? Have they agreed to be the stimulus that stops you being bored and boring?

There is no Grace in treating people like this. Better to part company than abuse them in this way.

Being in famine and down time can be frightening. Perhaps this is a time of no money, no work, no lover, no recognition, no acceptance for us. Despite what I have written, I know it is only human to wish for such times to pass and more happening times to come.

But don't overlook the fertility of the silent or empty times. There is much to learn in them and from them. Things aren't as non-moving as they appear to be. Seeds of the plants that will provide food for the next feast are already germinating in the dark.

Make sure the ground in which they have been conceived is healthy and rich enough to sustain the growth of the next happening that will eventually come your way.

You, your heart, mind, body and spirit should lie quietly like the seeds in the ground. Equanimity and trust in the face of not knowing for sure that anything good will ever happen to you again, is the enrichment required.

* Everything living moves in cycles of nothing/something. It is the same with you and your life.

* When the things you need to happen don't, take what action you can to move your situation forward, then leave it to shift itself in good time.

* Don't spend down time panicking. Spend it growing calmer so that good ideas can grow in a still mind.

* Don't use other people to fill up your empty times. This is not what friends are for. Friends are a feast in themselves and time spent with them should be celebrated as the best of times.

Notes:

32. Do you play, 'they love me, love me not'?

Doesn't it feel really great when people appreciate you, think you're talented and want more of your company?

Well doesn't it?

But doesn't it feel worrying when you realise that something you've said or done apparently has lost you all that good will and praise. Suddenly you become much less acceptable to others.

Why do people do this to you? Perhaps the important question is why do you allow it?

'But,' you may say, 'I haven't done anything. One minute they love me and the next minute they love me not.' It all feels so out of your control doesn't it?

The real problem is that you gave your power away. You invested too much value in others' good opinion of you and when you no longer have that, your investment seems valueless.

If it were your money you were investing and you were advised that if you went ahead you would be as likely to lose it as make a profit because of the instability of the market, as likely as not you wouldn't do it.

It's just as precarious when you invest in the opinions of other people. They are inconsistent in their views and change, sometimes for reasons that are nothing to do with you whatsoever. Often people appear to have changed their minds about you because of something totally unconnected with you: their lives, what sort of a day they're having, whether they got out of bed the wrong side that day.

Why trust something so unstable, so changeable, so little to do with you and so based on someone else's feelings of the moment?

(However, this doesn't mean that we should ignore compassionate feedback from those few people we have come to trust).

But even better still, try to gain a Graceful and balanced view of yourself, your strengths and weaknesses, the areas you are proud of and the personal things you are hoping to change.

* We all have our blind spots, but usually when we are calm and centred, our own opinion of ourselves has validity.

* Don't let non-appreciation from others take away your pleasure. People have opinions as surely as night follows day.

* Receive positive opinions Gracefully but with balance, consider negative opinions to check out their truth in your own experience. Then breathe out and get on with your day.

Notes:

33. Will the real you please stand up?

* Is there a you that the people at work know?

* Is there another you that the people at home know?

* Do some friends know yet another you?

* Would others not recognise any of these yous, but know a different person entirely?

* Do you find yourself using different voices or different ways of speaking in different places?

Well, who is the real you? Or is it that they are all part of the real you and you aren't brave enough to get them all together at any one time with everyone you know?

Mmm, this is a serious matter.   What we are discussing is your ability to be authentic.

Being authentic is really about being real everywhere. Being inauthentic is about projecting out a you that you believe will be acceptable in a given situation. Those projections can be a habit that becomes permanent so that a person can never really feel always themselves in any area of their lives.

You can test out the extent to which this is happening in your life by answering a few questions:

* Would you feel comfortable having all the people you know in one room observing you? Would you know which you (which set of behaviours, mannerisms and voices) to be?

* If all the people you knew were in a room with you (work colleagues/family/friends/partners) and you had to decide just one way to be, which group would be most surprised as they watched and listened to you?

* When you answer the phone expecting a call from a work colleague and a friend answers, are they initially unsure they are talking to you or do they ever comment on how different you sound?

* What would it be like if you couldn't turn the different yous on and off at will? What embarrassments could occur?

All this switching between your yous puts a strain on your real self: the one who has decided to be the director. This director has arranged for actors to play multiple roles in order to be acceptable everywhere.

Learning to be an actor starts very early in life when we suddenly realise that being our natural, Gracefully beautiful and authentic selves everywhere is not always appreciated by the people in charge of us. We find this unloving response confusing, saddening and frightening and because we are resourceful, we try to find ways to conform in order to be loved.

We soon find that no one set of conforming behaviours will please all the people all the time. To manage this we develop different sets of behaviours and ways of being; a bit like having a variety of clothes to wear for different occasions. When this happens, what is being covered up is the natural truth of what and who we are.

It is heartbreaking to have our real selves unappreciated. The cost to us is our authenticity – the real us goes into hiding just in case we make a 'mistake' and become painfully unacceptable.

We lose sight of ourselves and often have a permanent feeling of anxiety, being a fraud or experiencing an underlying fear of discovery and exposure.

Have you ever thought to yourself, 'if you knew what I was really like, you wouldn't employ me/be my friend/love me,'?

But you will never know the truth behind that question unless the you that isn't assuming a role begins to be the you that lives your life for you and with you.

How unsatisfactory will it be at the end of your life to realise that no-one had really known the whole you because you had only shown each person one part of you at a time?

Will the real you please stand up while there is still time?

Begin to be braver. Collect up your many selves and take them out into the world together. Give yourself and the world a real treat!

Notes:

34. How much certainty do you need?

In modern life we have got used to needing what appears to be a high degree of certainty about almost everything.

We can prevent this, enable that, stop things, make things happen. Somehow we can get the feeling that we are infallible. However, running alongside this, people often seem to have an underlying anxiety that is hard to name. If we really are able to be in control of most things why are we so worried?

Of course the truth is that the idea of humanity being in control is an illusion. This illusion is a destructive one because while we have it, we never stop to think about what there is that we **can** be sure of. After all, who is it that we depend on for this control that we allow to reassure us: the government, the army, the doctors, some other nameless institution.

Of course they can't. No one group, no matter how powerful they seem, can arrange things for us so that we are permanently safe. A sense of safety can only come from within ourselves. To really know this is a scary but liberating thing.

Our sense of safety comes from a realistic view of what life is about with its birth, and death cycles. We live in a body that doesn't last for ever, so sooner or later we or our loved ones will get sick and die. Reading this you might say, 'why would I want to live with this gloomy prospect constantly uppermost in my mind.'

A sense of personal safety comes from being in touch with the reality of being human, doing what you can to enhance the quality of your life by taking care of yourself and your loved ones sensibly, and getting in touch with the creative life force that animates you and all other living things.

This life force (which you may know as intelligence, spirit, God, Goddess or some other Holy Name) is the source of all things and has provided the Grace you call your existence so far. It is far more dependable than the stock market or the government. It will provide you with safety and peace of mind if you let it.

* When you sit quietly, try to be still and make contact with your own life force. Feel the buzz or vibration of life running beneath your skin.

* If you are anxious or feeling unsafe, ask life to take these feelings away from you and request instead to receive peace of mind.

* When a problem arises in your life, do all you can to improve your situation, then ask for guidance.

* Remember that the life force in you is the same One that is in everyone and everything else, so no matter how alone you feel with your trouble, you never are.

* Don't depend on other manmade control mechanisms more than is sensible. Find a quiet courage within yourself and you will become as certain as you will ever need to be.

Notes:

35. What are you doing with your greatest strength?

We all know what we're good at. Sometimes we know what we would like to be better at too. We don't always realise that our greatest strengths are often our weaknesses taken to excess. Are you like this?:

For example, to some of you, doing a perfect job; getting everything done to your specification is a great strength. Other people can rely on you to do things to the very best of your ability. The downside is that sometimes you can be pedantic, insisting that things have to be done a certain way and that your way is best.

Do you love to help others, seeing what they need without asking, giving up your time generously to make things alright for other people? This works very well until they don't need your help any more or don't feel as dependent on you as they once did and then you feel hurt or discarded. It may be that the 'after all I've done for you' feeling rises in you?

Perhaps you love to set goals, go for it, succeed wherever possible out in the world and build up a reputation for this. In order to do this though, you may become whatever is required to succeed, losing the real you in the process.

Others love to feel special, to imitate and reproduce the artistic and the unusual to achieve this. If this is you, do you over dramatise your situation, often despairing of feeling accepted and loved for just who you are without acting.

Maybe you are one of those people who love acquiring knowledge, facts and always read the computer manual from beginning to end. Everyone will come to you when they want to know how to do something, but sometimes facts will be all you have to offer: the real you, the human being, just isn't available to be in relationship with.

* You aren't only the thing you do best. You are many different skills and attributes.

* Don't be so proud of what you do well that you allow others to know you only on that basis.

* Some of the most interesting things about people are their incompetences. Bring yours out of the cupboard more often.

* Consider other peoples' skills. Where would you benefit from learning something new and learning it in a new way?

* Don't be afraid to surprise others. Let them see the other you that wants to learn.

Notes:

36. Do you believe there won't be enough?

Have you seen the queues at the supermarket before Christmas, Thanksgiving or other public holidays? What can we make of the loaded trolleys: does everyone have six children and a huge extended family to prepare meals for?

Does the sight of such consumerism ever strike you as obscene in contrast to the reportage in the media of those with nothing, or of the of street people with a blanket and a dog?

Why do we hoard as if there was never going to be another opportunity to get what we need?

Perhaps we are programmed with a fear of lack and a distrust of the idea that there is enough for all of us to get our needs met.

For some of us, we inherited this fear from our families as we were growing up and have taken it on board in our own lives, no matter what our present circumstances may be.

For others, enough is never enough, no matter how the cupboards, wardrobes, bank accounts bulge, nor how many friends and lovers we have – and it never will be.

Impoverishment is not only a physical state of hardship existing in world's poor places – it is rife as a mental concept in the minds of many of us living in some of the most affluent places too.

What about you?

How much is enough anyway?

Suppose, just for a few minutes (if that's all we can manage), we considered 'enough' as just a fraction more of anything that we really need to support our chosen lives at any given moment.

If you could accept that definition, how would it change your idea of how blessed you are in terms of having enough of what is necessary for you?

For 'just enoughness' to work for you, an important something else must be added. This something else is your ability to trust that the next portion of enough would be provided or put your way.

This is where the definition of just enoughness I have suggested begins to give some people a problem. It can be very difficult to have faith that the small amount you have in excess of your actual need will be replenished. This difficulty of faith can result in people beginning to operate a 'just in case' strategy rather than a 'just enough' one.

It is 'just in caseness' that causes us to over stock on almost everything and a lack of faith in natural abundance (there is enough for all of us) that prompts that reaction in us.

So whether having a pound or a dollar more than you need in your purse or wallet enables you to feel well off, or whether even a million in your bank account, still can't stop you from needing to accumulate more, your belief or non-belief that your needs will be met is at the root of your abundance strategy.

* Take some time to consider the natural world and how the notion of abundance works there.

* Do you believe that anything outside yourself or your own will power will enable you to survive and get what you need? If so what?

* Do you operate from an idea of poverty or an idea of abundance? If you oscillate between the two, where and how do you feel most Graceful?

* If you have over-accumulated things/possessions/money/stuff, what do you hope will happen to it when you die?

* If you could have only five possessions in your life, what would they be?

Practice considering yourself as Graced with natural abundance. See what difference that makes to your life.   What have you got in your cupboard and accounts now?

Notes:

37. Do you enjoy gossiping and moaning?

Does it all spill out of your mouth as soon as you get anywhere near a friend or an acquaintance?

Do you talk about others behind their backs?

Perhaps it's your sad story you talk about: the things that are going wrong in your life that you simply have to share.

What is this need that many human beings have to moan about others or about our own lives.

What need does this fulfil in us?

Is it a desire to find some sort of closeness or intimacy with others by comparing personal difficulties? Do we hope to find agreement from others on our views about third parties not present?

Perhaps there is a better way to fulfil this need without resorting to moaning. Moaning can be a habitual thing: something that happens when we have finished saying, 'Hello, how are you?' and before we say 'Goodbye, take care.'

Next time you spend pleasant minutes gossiping with someone, spend time afterwards, when you are on your own, trying to recall what you both said.

* Was any of it really worth saying?

* Have you had identical conversations with others recently? Were you just repeating yourself to yet another person and going through your 'broken record' technique?

* Did you say something about someone else that damaged their reputation, even in a small way?

* Did you listen to someone else damaging another's reputation and join in?

* What was there, if anything, that you really wanted to say but didn't?

Take care that your mouth has not become a disgraceful weapon of mass destruction: blaming, complaining, disbelieving, twisting facts to suit your purposes, lying, bringing down others and cynically taking the joy out of others' experiences.

The complex development of the faculties of speech and comprehension in human evolution could be a gift of great Grace to us. Try considering what comes out of your mouth as sacred. See if this makes a difference to what you wish to say.

Notes:

38 Do you frighten yourself with all you have to do?

Sometimes it's easy to wear yourself out with thinking about all you have to do in a day, instead of just doing it.

Thinking forwards through the day, the week or the next month and wondering how you will fit it all in is exhausting. This isn't the same as planning. Planning is necessary in a busy life. Once you have made your plan, know where you are going, what you have to prepare, what you have to take with you, what clothes, papers, tools, knowledge, have to be clean and ready etc., you stop looking forward and start being present.

In our imaginations, all we have to do looms large and impossible, whereas it is possible to achieve a lot if you aren't constantly preoccupied with the next thing you have to do instead of concentrating on the thing you are doing now.

I expect you know how this rushing forward state looks in somebody else. Perhaps you are having a conversation with someone when their eyes glaze over, their responses become mechanical and although their body is still standing before you, their mind has gone somewhere else.

Who is on the receiving end of that distracted state when you do it? I wonder how they feel about that?

Give each thing you have to do 100% of your attention. Move on to thinking about the next thing when you have finished. If a thing is not worth 100% of your attention, then don't do it at all.

When you feel yourself drifting towards the next place in your mind, when you are still engaged in the task or the interaction before, bring yourself back to the present.

Sometimes we find that this level of attention is just not possible, because we have no emotional investment in what we are doing. We just don't care about it. If too much of your life is spent doing things you just don't care about, it is time to rethink the situation.

After all, what you do with or in your life is your life. Why waste it on things and people that don't interest you?

* How much of your life is spent doing things you don't care about?

* If you can't change that completely (or don't think you can) can you decrease the percentage of waste?

* Who or what are you most passionate about?

* How can you increase your life's investment in these things or people?

* Don't worry about how much you have to do. Just do it.

Live your life as if you really cared what you did with it. Don't worry so much. Take action. Live.

Notes:

39. Do you take prisoners?

How many prisoners have you currently got locked up inside of you?

Your prisoners are all the people you can't let go of, can't forget, can't or won't forgive. You carry them around with you all the time, housing them and feeding them with your energy.

Every now and again you let them up into your mind or your heart to take a little exercise while you review the case against them.   Are they suitable for parole? Can you yet let them go?

But they hurt you, left you or forgot you didn't they?. Their crimes against you eat away at your peace, happiness and your ability to move on. How could they have treated you like that? How can you consider letting them go when you want to punish them for what they have done to you?

Perhaps you feel you should keep them locked inside with your bitterness for ever.

Eventually when the prison that is yourself becomes full of inmates, you might persuade someone else to house a few of them for you. If you tell your friends and loved ones about how badly you've been treated, they may agree to hold some of your bitterness against that person too. That will spread the load quite nicely.

It might be time to consider the cost of all this to you.

Have you ever been in a real prison? The bitterness, anger and desire for revenge is palpable. Is that what you want to become? To hold dark and negative thoughts trapped inside you.

* Begin to let your prisoners go. Whatever they did and however that felt, it is now in the past. Don't make it your present and future for the rest of your life.

* Decide what to do with the energy that will be freed up when you forgive your prisoners and set them free

* Write a letter to your prisoner. Tell them you are now just fine as you are: no longer feel angry, sad or hurt and saying goodbye. Send it if you can, but if you can't burn it and as the smoke rises, remember that as you set them free, you free yourself as well.

Open all the cell doors in your heart. Let all the prisoners go and start to live again.

Notes:

40. Hush, be quiet

What do you do when you have a problem or something worrying you about your life? Perhaps you talk to a friend about it and get their advice? Some of us might go to a specialist and pay for being told what to do? Others will just worry the difficulty round and around in their heads, hoping to come to a good conclusion.

Often there is no clear answer to the problem or situation that is going round and round in our minds. We may think we know what the right solution is or we may not know what 'should' happen at all. Either way, the talking, moaning, thinking and processing of our difficulty takes over our waking hours in an almost obsessive way.

One thing that has really surprised me is an ability to come to a reasonable solution apparently without talking or thinking about it very much at all. How does this work? Can you do this?

There seem to be several stages to this resolving process. This is what works for me:

1. Doing some basic thinking about the part I play in my own problem/situation. Getting clear about what I have invested in having the problem there in my life at all.
What does it give me?

2. Understanding what the problem really is rather than what it appears to be then simplifying it until it can be written down in one simple sentence

3. Realising that there is probably no one outcome that is better than any other although it might feel that way

4. Taking what action I can and then handing it over to the Universe, through prayer or some other 'asking' method

5. Letting the problem go and getting on with the rest of my life

6. Noticing that things are resolving themselves without interference

from my thinking mind

7. Being meticulous in observing changes happening and my own attitudes changing

8. Being grateful

We are so addicted to problem solving, debating, self-improvement and thinking that we have the grand idea that we can fix it all.

Life has been keeping itself together for a very long time despite our interference and ignorance. It has a virtue and a rightness all of its own. We are part of that healing consciousness. The right things are not necessarily the things we think we need. By doing what we can in our lives and handing over the things that we can't, we tap into a wisdom and justice that is far beyond our own limited understanding.

This transformational process is our birthright as living beings - and cheaper than all those sleepless nights and visits to a therapist!

Notes:

41. How do you manifest your life?

Everything in your life begins as a thought vibration.

How mental energy eventually turns itself into our physical reality is part of the Great Mystery that life is. We don't necessarily need to understand it, (although some metaphysicians and mages do), but just to notice that we get more of what we concentrate on, be it positive or negative.

How our life feels to us has much more to do with what we think about it than what our external circumstances dictate.

If we feel satisfied inside with the external state of things, we lead a satisfied life no matter what physically happens to us.

If we feel we lead an unsatisfactory existence, our many blessings, friends and belongings won't make a bit of difference to our dissatisfaction.

* What do you think about your own life?

* How is what you predominantly think mirrored out there in your own life?

* Have you always supposed that your external life comes first and your thoughts follow on after?

* Begin to notice how your life seems to confirm your predominant thoughts.

If you want, you can begin to think and feel exactly as you would like to. Your inner feelings are not as connected to your circumstances as you have supposed. It is only you who has decided to connect them up in the way that you do.

There is a great Graceful freedom in making a separation between how you think and feel and what is happening 'out there'.

Although we can't always control what happens to us in our lives, we aren't obliged to think or feel anything we don't wish to.

This takes discipline and practice, but sets us free to remain calm and present no matter what is happening in our lives.

* Try it. The next time something doesn't go smoothly, don't indulge in 'it's all going wrong' thinking.

* Observe what has happened, take action where you can and continue to enjoy your day. Don't become fixated on the 'wrongness' in your life.

You lead a happy life when you think and feel you do, not when outward conditions dictate.

Notes:

42. Can you do straight talking?

Can you do straight talking? Straight talking is rather like straight walking in that you take a clear and simple direction from where you are to where you want to be, but in words rather than steps.

Straight talking is communicating without undue emotion: passing information to another person in such a way that they understand what it is you want to say.

Often the most difficult things to talk about straightly arise when strong emotions are involved. Quite often we avoid telling another person that they have upset us or made us angry because we don't know what to do if they don't respond 'well'.

Instead we show them that we are angry or upset instead of telling them. This may sound the same to you but is very different.

It is also much less effective. We may believe that others can be in no doubt about our angry feelings, but often this is not the case. Viewed from the outside our anger could look like sadness, distractedness or indigestion. The cause of that feeling could be no-one in particular, shoes that are too tight or something or someone unknown.

It is surprising how often people can be completely unaware of the effect of their behaviour on us. If someone else's behaviour has upset or hurt you, especially if it happens often, then it is worth drawing it to their attention using straight speaking.

So how do you do this?

* Begin by explaining simply and clearly what it was that the other person did or said that hurt you or made you angry.

* Don't speak to them angrily: instead tell them that you are angry in as balanced or centred a way as you can manage. Be brief and explicit about the behaviour you are complaining about and ask that they don't repeat it.

* When you've done that, be quiet and wait for a response.

What will happen next?:

* You may get an apology and a more productive conversation may follow.

* They may say they are surprised at your reaction and/or deny their treatment of you.

* They may believe you are too sensitive and should grow a thicker skin.

* They may laugh and say they were only joking.

* They may repeat the previous unhelpful behaviour.

Don't let any of the above move you from your centred position. Breathe deeply and repeat your request that they improve their treatment of you.

If they continue to argue or attempt to beat down your view, end the conversation with a request that they think about what you have said and walk away.

Don't be discouraged if you don't get a satisfactory response immediately. What you have said might take a while to have an effect. Everyone learns in their own time and some lessons are harder to learn than others. Be patient.

Surprisingly, the criteria for success when you straight talk is not that you get an apology, get the other person to agree with you or even really to hear you, although it's great when this happens.

It's certainly not about getting your own back or making the other person feel bad. It's about regaining your dignity and communicating how you wish to be treated. It's also to do with feeling good about yourself.

It's a much more graceful habit to be able to communicate your negative or strong feelings calmly and directly to the appropriate person, rather than dumping them on your partner, work colleagues or going home and kicking the cat!

Unless you enjoy your suffering, it makes sense to attempt to resolve difficulties with other people promptly, otherwise negative feelings turn inwards and undermine your precious sense of self worth.

It takes a little courage to begin talking straight, but the payoff in terms of your self-esteem makes it well worthwhile to have a go.

Notes:

43. Do you leave what is most important until last?

Why is it that we often leave the most important people or things until last on our list of things to attend to?

What is it that makes us use the best of our energy and most of our valuable time on things that don't matter much at all?

Perhaps we haven't taken the trouble to work out what is most important to us. If this is you, it's easy to work out whether or not something is important to you by imagining what would happen if this person or that thing were not in your life. Would it matter? Would you care a little or a lot? The answers should give you the level of value of this in your life.

Maybe we know which things and people are most important and are waiting to make absolutely certain that we know exactly and precisely what to do before we act.

Planning and checking and replanning and rechecking every little detail before taking action is often another avoidance and one that can be used indefinitely

If you have many things to do, getting a few quick wins is very tempting to clear a few items off the to-do list. But doing unimportant or easy things first can also be another way of avoiding the real issues.

If you are still having trouble prioritising and taking action, it might be worth applying the following to each thing on your to do list.

* Ask yourself what will happen if you don't take action soon on each item on your to-do list.

* Is it **a.** improbable, **b.** likely or **c.** inevitable that that there will be negative consequences as a result of your non-action?

* Then consider that if those negative consequences do occur, will they be **1** of little significance, **2.** worrying, or **3.** devastating to you?

Items on your list that you have scored as having inevitably devastating consequences for you obviously require immediate action.

* look at how you avoid taking action and why

* be clear about the real consequences of putting things off

* do first things first. The cost of doing first things last is too great!

Notes:

44. Can you let it be?

Can you let it be, leave it alone, cease interfering with it?

The **it** can be anything from your partner or your child to the garden or your health. Sometimes we believe that if we don't alter, push, control or change things, they will never improve: never be right.

Some people appear to have a mission in life to attempt to improve everyone and everything.   If you do this, improvement is likely to mean improved in your opinion and to your criteria for what 'better' looks like.

There is a wonderful Grace in lovingly accepting others for who and what they are without the impertinence of constant correction and complaint.

Anxious mothers constantly correct their little ones with 'no', 'don't do that', 'that's not nice', 'that's naughty'. Obviously, for the child's own safety the parents must sometimes intervene, but constant advice and correction eventually falls on deaf ears as the toddler switches off to the endless stream of demands and corrections.

Children are born with the belief in their own perfection. Consider the number of depressed and troubled adults in the world who feel anything but perfect. How did they come from that Graceful state of innocence and belief in themselves to having little confidence in their ability to love and be loveable?

If our parents and carers constantly corrected and attempted to control our behaviour, our sense of perfection is soon replaced with a sense of wrongness. They were not able to just love us and let us be. They had no faith that we would, with loving kindness and guidance, grow up strong and true. The choice we have then is to believe them and become passive in our grief for the loss of our own perfection, or rebel in an attempt to hold on to our real selves in the face of overwhelming opposition.

This is not to blame our parents for the way we are: they did their best (most of them), it just wasn't always the best for us despite their best intent (as they saw it).

Think about falling in love. We set eyes on our beloved and notice all the unusual and fascinating things about them that make them so different from us and therefore desirable. How long is it before these beautiful differences become sources of irritation that we simply have to change or correct. We often end up leaving a lover for the reasons that drew us towards them in the first place. We simply cannot let them be. We know what they should be like; how they should behave. We are convinced they should be different to the way they are.

How can deep and real love last in the face of such abuse? How hurtful is it to feel that your lover would love you if only you were more like them or different to the way you are? Why can't they let you be and love you for the way you are?

Consider this:
* Not everything can be improved by our interference. In these cases it's us that needs to change, not the other.

* Only take on battles with your loved ones when not to do so would result in serious consequences. Otherwise practice distracting, (especially in the case of children), laughing, teaching by example, 'getting off it' and letting be.

* Children and adults change naturally and easily when they are given a loving example and Graceful acceptance. Demands for change simply produce resistance and resentment in healthy human beings large or small.

Notes:

45. Is the clock in your head running slower than your watch?

Some of us are always late and often keep others waiting. Apart from this we may be reliable people who generally believe we keep our agreements with others. Perhaps our relationship with linear time is compromised in one way or another.

Why might this be:
• Because we believe that it is very important to do things to our own timescales. We may be blissfully unaware that others are being kept waiting or we know this and don't find it as important as our own priorities.

• We constantly underestimate the amount of time it takes to do anything or arrive anywhere.

Tardy people usually have a collection of justifications for wasting others' time.
a. types might say:

* my workload is so heavy/my schedule is so crammed (as if this is something out of their control) – (and possibly they don't say but mean: I have to do so much more than you or more than you realise).

The conscious or unconscious inference here is that what I have to do is more important than your time which we both know I have wasted by keeping you waiting.

The underlying principle might well be, 'I care more about my time than yours and I am justified in doing so because of my priorities'.

b. types might say:

* goodness me is that the time. I didn't realise – I looked at the clock and I couldn't believe how late I had got – and then the traffic........

The suggestion here is that they are completely at the mercy of time, which conspires against them and prevents them from fulfilling the agreement to meet with you at the appointed hour. The inference is that they ought to be absolved of responsibility for being late because something out of their control prevented them from being on time.

The underlying principle might be that 'this is the way it is and there isn't much I can do or say about my lateness', (and you should understand my problem and make allowances for it).

Whatever the reasons for habitual lateness, it wastes one of the other's most valuable resources: their linear time which measures out of the hours of their lives.

It is also a control mechanism, putting the latecomer in charge and giving the one waiting very few choices: to continue waiting or not; to be angry or not.

So if lateness is a habit for you, what can you do to improve your relationship with time:

* Investigate time management strategies and find one that works for you

* Become a more effective prioritiser. Do first things first. If the person you are keeping waiting is not one of your top priorities and other things are, tell them and don't arrange to meet them. (Don't use people to fill the gaps between your priorities).

* Decide what it says about you when you break the agreements you have made with others

* Consider what it means to keep agreements

* Check out your delusions of grandeur: 'my life/time/work/schedule is more important than yours', type thinking

* Become more realistic about how long things take

Linear time itself is probably an illusion and a way of making pure spacious infinity less frightening. But as we have all colluded and agreed to use it, let's make it work for us in a disciplined and Gracious manner.

(We have all agreed to use it haven't we?)

(Do I hear someone over there saying, 'No!)?

Notes:

46. You can be what you love

We are told a lot about what we are and what we are supposed to
be. We are even told that we are what we eat! Sometimes it can
become infuriating to be told who and what we are by others. At
the risk of infuriating you further, I would like to suggest that you
spend a few minutes considering that you may be or could become
what you most love.

One of the most amazing features of our soulfulness is that it is
infinitely impressionable and influenced by our life's experience. At
least it is if we are open to that.

Sometimes we become so tight and closed that nothing leaves its
mark on us. We may even say, 'you won't change me,' to life, as if
we were entering a competition to remain exactly as we are from
now until eternity. This closedness is usually the result of emotional
pain and fear.

Yet whether we are aware of it or not, what we crave most is
change, variety and exposure to otherlyness. This provides the
stimulus for our inquiry; our term of growing and expanding. We
cannot stimulate ourselves towards our unknown potential when we
have nothing new in ourselves to stimulate ourselves with, until we
allow something novel and outside us, in.

With just a little courage and help, we can reopen to the new, the
strange and the lovely.   The soul is impressioned most readily by
the things we find beautiful; the things we love.

When we experience a clear, star filled night, a newborn baby, a
pounding ocean, the forest, a flower, our child sleeping, a wonderful
painting, ecstatic music, tender poetry, making love deeply, having
conversations with the Source of all things or creating something
beautiful, our soul allows us to become that experience.

Have you ever felt that you were becoming a sunset as you watch
the sun go down. Why does the beauty of such things move you to
tears? The deep shift from looking at something outside you and

feeling that experience move you and change you on the inside, is part of your process of becoming what you love. The more you allow yourself time to reflect with Grace on the things and people that you love, coming to an understanding of their essence, the more they become part of you. The impressions of your soul, become manifested in your self; in your life.

Alternatively, you could choose to allow the impressions you gather to be dark and less loving. The soul is not drawn to these in the same way, as it is attracted by the beautiful. But the choice is yours. You could become what you most love or what you most hate.

* What opens your heart? Spend time with these impressions. Allow them to change you.

* What closes your heart? Take action when you must, but don't dwell there. Join with your soul in celebrating your own becoming - as Graceful beauty and love.

Notes:

47. Are you a puppet on a string....

...being pulled about by your emotions? Do you feel you have a choice about first feeling and being pulled this way and then feeling and being pulled that way?

The problem with being emotional creatures is that most of us don't use our emotions in the way we could. Emotions are to alert us to what is going on inside: to inform us and help us to be more intelligent about our own state. They were never intended to take us over.

Our response mechanism to our emotions is, for the most part, a reaction. Sometimes this reaction is so swift that it by-passes mind. Such reactions are often unintelligent and leave us feeling taken over and out of control.

A reaction such as this often brings with it all sorts of unresolved troubles from the past, so what we say and do at these times is probably not about what is going on in the present at all, but simply triggered by it.

Whoever is on the receiving end of such a reaction is left wondering what on earth is happening and why. It's a bit like lighting a fuse and watching a firework go off and of course, this tendency in some people can be manipulated deliberately by others with their own agenda.

Attempting to become like a robot – without emotions – is not the answer, nor is just allowing others to treat you badly while you sit passively by. The answer is to feel and recognise the emotion without adding a reaction to it, or at least until you are ready and decide to do so with balance and Graceful wisdom.

How can you begin to be slower to react:

* First of all recognise the emotion and decide exactly what it is trying to tell you. If you believe that the emotion is trying to tell you

something about someone else, you are mistaken in your interpretation of its message. If you think that the emotion is just telling you something about now, check it out: what does the present situation raise for you in terms of the past?

* Become aware of what the emotion is saying about **you.** No-one can ever make you unhappy/angry/afraid but yourself. The feelings we get are our reactions to what is going on outside us. The emotion is telling you that something is happening outside you that you would not choose and that the feeling self has been alerted by this.

* Because we are feeling creatures, it is right that we become aware of the strength and depth of our emotions and the physical expression of them. So name them and thank them for the information about you that they give, take responsibility for them and know that they are to do with you and no-one else. Then let them pass through you – with humour or sadness as necessary and let them go.

This kind of intelligence raises our human state up a notch. Just watch someone who has completely suppressed their emotions. They seem only partly alive.

Again, observe someone who has completely lost their temper. They appear to be at the mercy of their emotions (the puppeteer) and show little Grace or intelligence in their responses.

Who are you allowing to pull your strings? Cut yourself free and stand firmly at the centre of yourself.

Notes:

48. You are a Universe

You are not only a Universe, but also a self-organising one at that.

You are planets, stars, gas, water and rock. Without your help your cells are born and die, your organs do the job they do, your brain sends millions of impulses around your body and your great heart beats without you having to lift a finger.

Do you ever thank your body for what it does for you and marvel at it? Perhaps what you do mostly, is to blame it for what it doesn't do and doesn't look like.

Just for now, let's consider our bodies with love; as the miraculous universe that they are. Try this:

* light a candle and sit comfortably. Feel your breath rise and fall inside your chest without trying to change it.

* consider the idea of inner space. Work around the inside of your head getting a sense of the spaciousness between your eyes and the open spaces in your skull.

* Hum and hear the resonance and vibration in your sinuses.

* Breathe again deeply and feel your lungs expand. Picture the air filling even the tiny spaces inside them.

* Voyage around your inner universe. Explore using the lymph system or your veins and arteries as your route. See what you find.

You are a universe filled with hard matter, soft, expanding bodies, liquid and air. Everything is coming together, moving, parting and remeeting in you. Even when things don't work in quite the way they could, the universe that is the body is a living miracle.

* What does inner space mean to you? Is it something you are conscious of as you go about your day?

* Become aware of the different sensations produced by your major organs. Often we only notice these when we are in pain. What does your stomach feel like? What about your spleen?

* Feel down into the inside of your feet, just inside the skin of the sole. What does the sensation of meeting the ground feel like for your feet?

When you are very still, notice the slight vibration just inside the outside of the body. This is the Life in you making itself felt. In this you share a legacy with every living thing. You are unique and yet there are so many of you!

Notes:

49. Linking yourself to then time and when time.

Our relationship with time is often that of a child with an over controlling parent; a parent that either rules us or one that we rebel against.

This way of being conscious of time deals pretty much with the present and represents our ability to be with time, Gracefully, or not as the case may be. But what about the past and the future (then and when time) and the thread of our existence that goes back into one (then) and forward into the other (when).

Our ancestors measure the length of this unbroken relationship with the past and unborn generations measure the way that the thread of our lives go forward. Both are present, right now in our inheritance and our potential. We owe respect, gratitude and occasionally apology to both.

Consider some of the decisions that modern man takes: to go to war, to leave some people without shelter or food, to poison the planet, to fill the body of the earth with rubbish in landfills. If we don't raise our voices and remain passive, then we have some explaining to do to those yet to be born who will be affected by what we have done and not done.

* Imagine that an ancestor was standing before you. Explain to him or her your stance on homelessness or the care of the elderly. Explain how, in your view, these social problems have come to be in our society and what you personally are doing about them. Tell them what you have done with the resources left to you by their generation and imagine their response.

* See a child from the future of your family. They are asking you questions about nuclear waste, landfill sites, birth defects caused by the poisoning of the atmosphere. They want to know why you personally did little and what you imagined their life would be like as a result of inaction. Explain to them why you did what you did, or didn't do. Take responsibility in your reply. Ask to be forgiven.

The past and the future are as alive in each moment as they were then and will again be. We are an integral part of everything our ancestors did and were and all that the future generations will become. We are not just about now.

Just about now time makes us small, finite and alone. It is an illusion and a shoving away of the responsibility and kinship with the thread of our lives from the past and the thread running into the future. It enables us to be the cause of suffering for those who will follow us. Is that the legacy you want to leave? Begin considering it now.

If everyone in the past had felt that way our lives would be less rich. Imagine those who designed and built wonderful architecture not bothering to do so because it probably wouldn't be finished in their own lifetime.

* What do you do that will benefit those to come?

* What do you do that you need to apologise for? Try writing a letter to the future to explain yourself.

Notes:

50. Can't decide? See what your body does

For some of us, making decisions and coming to conclusions about
what we should do is a very difficult process.

We weigh up the pros and cons interminably; checking and
rechecking the facts and the possible outcomes and we still can't
decide.

The problem is often that we believe that there is only one right
answer and we are afraid of the consequences of choosing the
wrong one.

There is often more than one thing we could do and sometimes, it
matters little what we do and is more important that we do
something. Doing something breaks the tension of not being able to
decide.

Sometimes doing nothing is just as effective and things choose
themselves or present themselves to be acted on. We find ourselves
acting on this, rather than that, and wonder about the thought
process that helped us make up our minds so subtly that we weren't
aware of it happening.

In these cases, what may have occurred, is that the body has made
up your mind, rather than you or your mind making up your mind.

The body appears to have a wisdom of its own that can be quite
overlooked in the decision making process. However we know very
well that the body is good at removing us from danger in a hurry
when it needs to and it will jerk our hand away from something that
is burning it. We call these decisions that the body makes reflex
actions and take it for granted that the body will keep us safe in
these ways.

But your body is capable of more than just knee jerk reactions. It
has a wisdom of its own from which you can benefit if you are willing
to begin to tune in to it. Test it out by trying this:

* You want a cup of tea. Should you go and make it now or wait until later. Sit still and see what the body does. It will either get up and make the tea or it won't. You don't have to make the decision in your mind.

* You can't decide whether to phone a friend. Should you or shouldn't you? See whether your body makes the call or not. Stay where you are and watch to see whether your body rises up from your chair and lifts the phone.

* You thought you had decided not to get up and go to a meeting. You are surprised to find yourself in the shower, getting dressed, going to the meeting after all. Your body decided that you should go.

Become more aware of what your body is urging you to do. This works with anything from deciding what to eat and how, to when to go out and when to stay in. Your body isn't just a lump of flesh and bone. It has an intelligence all of its own. Learn how to use your own marvellous body. If not you, then who?

Notes:

51. Do you live in defence mode?

Are you always on the look out for a put down? Do you detect a criticism behind every question? Perhaps you plan things carefully, anxious to spot a weakness in your ideas before anyone else points it out.

All this defending takes up our time and energy and yet we feel compelled to do it. We find ourselves justifying the way we've done things in case someone else thinks we are doing them wrongly.

Why does it matter so much what everyone else thinks of us and what we do? Why can't we just accept ourselves and our decisions and leave it at that?

Sometimes we will react to an anticipated criticism; a criticism that was never going to be made, taking an aggressive stance that puzzles and offends others. They will not understand that we have a scenario running through our minds and in this scenario it is vital that we are ready to defend ourselves against anyone who disagrees with us or what we do.

There are two linked themes operating when this happens:

* we aren't sure that who we are and what we do is ever really going to be good enough, no matter how we try, and we want to hide this from others if we can

* we are sure that other people will see that we aren't good enough, so we get ready to justify and defend ourselves (even though we believe they may be right).

In taking up this position, which we have been playing out since we were very young, we are making two mistakes that make us unhappy:

1. Seeing ourselves as flawed in some way is our first mistake. We are completely good enough and there is absolutely nothing to hide

2. because we believe others will see our imperfection, we look for evidence in what they say and do, that supports this belief. No matter what people actually say to us, we believe that we detect their disapproval. What we are determined to find we will, whether it is actually there or not.

In this way we have presented ourselves with a self-perpetuating difficulty, based on nothing but an erroneous idea of our own 'not good enoughness'. This idea grew inside us as a result of our interpretation of our world when we were too young to see the whole truth. So what can you do?

* stop feeding your feelings of not being good enough. It is making your life sadder and more difficult than it needs to be.

* stop blaming others for being critical of you. It is you that believe you are wrong, not them.

* spend time considering the idea of your own goodness and Grace. To do otherwise is a mistake and an insult to the Great Intelligence that created you perfect.

Notes:

52. Inner versus outer work

If you are a person that reflects, meditates, prays, sits with a teacher or guru, goes to church, synagogue or mosque, reads sacred literature or belongs to a spiritual group, the notion of inner work will be familiar to you.

The idea is that you become more awake, less deluded and take more personal responsibility for yourself in this life.

You may be someone who leads a busy life, goes to work, raises a family, gives charitably, grows a garden or produces art and music. You will understand the idea of outer work as becoming productive in your life.

You enjoy making certain things happen and consider these to be a measure of your effectiveness and skill in this life.

Some of you will try to keep both these modes of living and being in balance, giving time to outer work and giving attention to inner work also. If this is you, how does your inner work reflect your outer and vice versa.

If you have a hectic lifestyle, you might do your inner work at an ashram or other peaceful place. If your outer life is more measured, you might choose T'ai Chi or dance to get in touch with your spirit.

A difficulty can arise if your inner work is so different or alien from your everyday outer work, than one cannot flow into, nor affect the other.

Remember that the purpose of inner work is to create for us a more worthwhile and awake engagement with the world. If your inner work is appropriate, then your relationship with the outer world will be full of things that are worth attending to.

Many devotees who seek peaceful places as a temporary refuge from an over stuffed outer life, are actually taking a holiday, rather than a spiritual retreat. The test is how the learning impacts on life.

If you experience a peaceful glow that is hard to transport to outer work, or at best, lasts just a little while, it is possible that your inner versus your outer work, don't connect well enough with each other.

* What has your outer work got to do with your inner work? How do they affect one another?

* What has changed in your outer work as a direct result of your inner work and vice versa?

If you can find no correlation; if inner work is just a rest or a release from what you do out there in the world, be clear that you are simply taking a holiday.

There is nothing wrong with having a much needed break, but it may not give you the profound and deep feeling of connectedness with Grace that is truly nourishing and that will enrich what you do out there in the world. What inner work most clearly reflects your outer work? Rethink it.

Notes:

53. Being a grown up and having parents

Why is it that our parents continue to treat us in much the same way as they did when we were children?

And why do we continue to behave as we did when we were children to our parents?

The answer is complicated, but has a lot to do with habit. We are in the habit of treating people that we have a relationship with, in much the same way as we always did. Those people are in the habit of responding as they always have and on and on we go.

It's not that we don't try to update our behaviour, but that there is quite a lot of pressure and collusion to keep things the way they were; the familiar way when we all knew what to do and how to be.

This is why family gatherings at a wedding, a funeral or Christmas can be so uncomfortable for all concerned. The expectation is that we will all behave the same as we always did, knowing all the while that it is a sham. We are adults now, with our own families perhaps, but we still respond to our parents as if we were children and then blame them for it.

For their part, parents can see from the outside that their child is now an adult, but doesn't have the insider information that the adult child has about how different they now are. Parents can be stuck in an old recording of what to say and what to do.

Arguments and disagreements are sometimes the only way people have of breaking out of the old parent/child hierarchical routine. When disagreements occur, things are said and done in the heat of the moment that let parents know where they now stand. But this is a knee jerk reaction to a perennial problem. It is a cop-out where no-one involved is really taking responsibility for putting the relationship on a more respectful and appropriate footing. Such arguments break the tension for the moment, but feelings are hurt and no re-education process takes place. Nothing has changed. What can be done?

* Be kind, firm and consistent in not agreeing to play the child to your parents

* Speak to your adult children when you feel you don't know how to be with them any more. Ask them what they need from you now.

* Be clear and direct when something happens that doesn't reflect the relationship you now wish to have with your parents or your adult child.

* Be timely when something goes wrong. Speak up at the time. Don't leave things to fester.

* Put yourself in their shoes. What sort of relationship would you need if you were them? What would you hope for? What would you be afraid of?

A poor relationship with family members is a failure of Grace. Do what you can.

Notes:

54. Do you hate Christmas?

Do you hate the noise, the commercialism, the false jollity, the overeating and over drinking?

Perhaps you stay at home on Christmas day, not seeing anyone and not cooking the traditional meal.

Many people now feel this way as a kickback against the loss of meaning in Christmas and the other midwinter religious and spiritual festivals. Unfortunately, as most of those that are conscious of this loss are not now taking part, who is there to put things right?

It is easy to blame others for the way things have become at Christmas. But if we are aware of what is happening and just opt out, then we are more culpable than the over indulgers.

Like all living beings we feel the lack of light and warmth and therefore hope at wintertime. The midwinter festivals were intended to bring light, in one way or another, to people at the darkest and coldest times of the year.   Today this longing for light in the shortest days is represented by lights, candles and fires in the streets and in our homes.

The cynicism that some of us now have around Christmas saddens us inside, because there is something we genuinely miss about this festival that once gave us joy. If you look at small children meeting Christmas as a new event in their lives you can see what we have lost.

We have lost our innocence and wonder around Christmas and the disappointment of that makes us cynical.

Is it not possible to get back to that innocence in our adult approach to Christmas this year? There is much that is still worthwhile in the sharing of a meal, the giving of small gifts or cards and the bringing of the light into our homes.

We are completely in charge of whether other excesses mar this time of year for us. We don't have to take part in them, but we can't pretend they aren't happening either because we have taken part in the way things have come to be at Christmas. If you think Christmas is no longer as magical for you as it once was, change it.

* Prepare a magical and innocent time for yourself and your loved ones at Christmas.

* Don't sneer at others who overindulge: somewhere their desperation to feel happy and loved has taken an unhelpful route, that is all.

* Try not to opt out altogether as a reaction against commercialism at Christmas. You will be the one who misses out on simple pleasures and your gesture will go unnoticed.

Be peaceful at Christmas and extend your goodwill to all; even those who are loud, spend too much money or drink too much alcohol.

Notes:

55. Is it hard to start over again?

As I write today it is the first day of the New Year and for some, it is a time when we try to live up to the promises we make to be better, different, less habitual.

For many of the promisers, it can all feel rather daunting as they have made those promises or resolutions many times before and in many different guises without success. Why is it that when we set out with such good intentions, we are unable to keep to what we have promised ourselves and others that we will do?

Many of the resolutions we make are often about stopping things that we enjoy doing: eating, drinking, spending money. This may be one of the reasons that we fail. When we try to stop ourselves from doing what we enjoy, even when our excesses make us unhappy, we are playing the critical parent to our own rebellious child.

Many of us are programmed to dislike being told what to do, but will try our best to do it anyway. So many of our resolutions are doomed to fail because the parent in us criticises and the child in us finds ways to disobey.

When we try to start stopping things we enjoy all over again at the beginning of the New Year, we already know how to make ourselves fail and so we do. Each failure adds to our view of ourselves as quitters and makes the next attempt more likely to founder too.

How can we break the cycle of resolving and failing?

* make no public promises to stop this and that

* find one thing you would really like to do more of (rather than less of) and set a realistic and private goal.

* ensure that the thing you want to do more of is something that will have a major impact on your life.

* appreciate every incremental improvement you make

This way you begin to see yourself as someone who can make changes and improvements to your life when you wish to. Once you have confidence in your ability to change and start again, you will be able to tackle the more problematic issues without raising the opposition of the rebellious child in you.

Your desire to make improvements in the way you live your life is natural, human and good. Don't turn it into a reason to despair. For all the improvements you aren't yet able to make, there are many that you can. Put your attention on the achievable for now and the seemingly impossible will soon be within your power to shift. Think well of your efforts and know that soon, with a little work and a lot of patience, everything will be resolved.

Notes:

56. Are you policing your bad habits?

How many arrests have you made; how many convictions have you got? What sentences have you handed out to yourself?

What are your crimes? Are you addicted to this and that? Are your addictions and your bad habits constantly under the hammer of your judgement? Is this how you hope to rid yourself of them?

What are the things about you that make you deeply ashamed and filled with self-dislike? Do you hope to rid yourself of these imperfections by hating yourself?

How can this work when it is a lack of love, either real or perceived, that created these habitual ways of coping in the first place?

Our addictions are symptoms of our inability to really face up to ourselves and our situations, in a conscious and loving way. We tried to hide from ourselves, and the ways we used to do this – the numbing and the blurring – became our bad habits and our addictions.

Some of our addictions become such profoundly damaging symptoms, that our very existence is threatened and changed forever as a result. For those of us that are suspended in this alternative and dark reality, all compassion and peace be granted.

But for those who still have choice to choose, begin to explore the need to choose the cushion of coping rather than the unknown of living fully.

* What is the tension that rises in the body just before you reach for the credit card, the bottle, the chocolate or the joint? Try to catch it and name it before you try to obliterate it.

* Which of your senses clamours for peace just before the alcohol or the nicotine kicks in? What are you seeing, hearing or thinking that you must blot it out whenever you can?

* What is the need that is silenced and numbed by your bad habits? To be loved, to be found beautiful, to be included, to be successful, to like yourself?

Our bad habits are the symptoms of unsatisfied human needs. Perhaps if we put effort into finding out what we are really crying out for, there would be no need to use our habits to hide this from ourselves and others. We might discover that we are more Graceful than we knew.

* What do you do that you are ashamed of? Discover what you are attempting to cope with by doing it. Forgive yourself and see what happens next.

Notes:

57. Are you an emotional illiterate?

Why don't children have lessons on emotional literacy as well as reading, writing and arithmetic? Perhaps it's because many of us are not properly qualified to teach them?

Yet being emotionally illiterate, or unintelligent can wreak as much, if not more havoc in our lives than being unable to read or write.

Our emotions are the bridge between ourselves, our loved ones, our work and our world. They let us know what we feel inside about everything outside of us and provide us with a means of communicating ourselves to others.

Proper emotional 'education' gives us a language that enables us to share ourselves accurately and lucidly with others. Yet few of us receive such an education and do most of our emotional learning in those classrooms of hard knocks: the ups and downs of life. This is a bit like handing a young child an encyclopaedia when they have reached only a basic level of skill in reading and expecting them to be competent at dealing with it.

Being emotionally intelligent gets confused with the unfortunate habit that some people have of indiscriminately blurting feelings that have mounted up over time and explode like lava from a volcano all over the unsuspecting. This is what happens when people have been storing up feelings instead of dealing with emotions as they arise.   Culturally, this can provide ammunition for the non-emotional lobby to preach 'stiff upper lipness' as a better way of handling life's difficulties.

Those people who believe that they have the right to explode in feeling, pebble dashing everyone else in the process, do us no favours and give being emotionally intelligent a bad reputation.

How do we begin to improve our level of skill in using one of the most sophisticated systems for communication we have at our disposal:

* When others we are close to are feeling something deeply, help them to name what they are feeling. Don't close them down, say it could all be worse, there-there them or cheer them up. (When we do this we are simply trying to minimise our own discomfort at not being able to witness or be with their pain, not ours).

* Practice naming our own feelings as they arise (rage, simple sadness, happiness versus joy).

* Stay quietly with the feeling rather than acting it out in a physical way.

* Describe the feeling in words by telling someone who cares about you or write it down.

* If the exact name of the feeling is hard to find, persevere and it will become easier. You are probably just out of practice.

Simple steps like these start the process of undoing emotional illiteracy. If everyone joined in we could change the way we take part in our own society and thereby change our participation in our world.

Closer to home, we would be giving our children the precious gift of a literacy that could change and enhance their lives. Not to do so locks them and us inside ourselves with no graceful way of reaching out.

Notes:

58. Can you dare to do nothing?

Have you ever noticed that sometimes you go to bed fraught and worried about what to do to remedy a particularly difficult situation and when you wake, your mind has made itself up while you slept and everything is resolved in you? Apparently, you did nothing, but something happened nevertheless.

We simply cannot tolerate our own indecision or lack of action and have no trust that what we most need will be provided by life. All that is required is our cooperation. Somehow though, we cannot believe that life is that simple and need to rush about being clever. But why?

As a society, indecision and not knowing what to do can bring up feelings of powerlessness that we find hard to bear. We often spring into action – any action – to relieve ourselves of the tension caused by the powerlessness we are experiencing.

And yet in some ways, powerlessness is part of the truth and Grace of our human situation. We were born, with or without our consent as far as we can remember, and our bodies will die when the time comes. We have little power to prevent that, but we put that fact out of our minds and grab our power back by changing what we can change, collecting what we can collect and preventing what we can prevent while we are alive.

We seem to value 'getting into action' above doing nothing and letting things take their course.

* But what is it that we are supposed to be doing that is so much better than doing nothing?   And how do we know this is so?

Somehow, we give ourselves too much of a certain sort of power and fail to recognise the true power of our existence.

We buy things, get more stuff than we can use or store, compete with others for the best this and that, learn more about everything and anything – but in order to do what; be what? When we have finished doing all that (and we will be finished, no matter what we do), what will we have and be then? These things make us feel powerful at the time we get or do them, but that feeling doesn't last because it isn't real. Why do we do this over and over again?

Because we don't see the simple beauty in what we are, without doing anything at all. We simply can't believe that we, as we are, are IT. And in that disbelief we miss the point of our existence.

Notes:

59. Feeling overwhelmed by all there is to do?

When we think of all we have to do in one big lump, we often feel overwhelmed and decide to do nothing at all.

Consider redecorating a room in your house for example. It's easy and good fun to choose paint or wallpaper, think about whether the old curtains would do or would have to be replaced and imagine what rugs or lamps you would like to complete the new room.

Somehow though, you never quite get started. You think about it a lot, but don't actually begin. The more you think, the more overwhelmed by the thought of beginning you are. Moving the furniture, rubbing down the walls, vacuuming up the dust and covering up the floor, seem to be too time and energy consuming to make a start. You put it off for another time when you have a clear week in your diary. You are too busy and too tired to consider doing it now after all.

What is the process of initially wanting to decorate the room and feeling inspired to do it, then losing energy and finding excuses not to start the work at all.

We bring ourselves to the point of overwhelm by thinking of the job as a whole, not as a series of stages in a process. If we can't see ourselves finishing it, we can't make a start. We defeat ourselves and make ourselves tired without ever lifting a finger.

If you have something large and potentially overwhelming to do, consider it in ten minute slots. (I once climbed a mountain in the Himalayas using this strategy, so I know that it works). Think of the what you can and will achieve in the next ten minutes and nothing more. At the end of that ten minutes, renegotiate the next ten minutes until enough has been done for one day. Don't think about one moment that is outside the next ten minutes. This way the fearful one inside you is fooled and won't start worrying about failure or exhaustion or whatever other excuse it gives you not to do.

This is much the same principle as living life one day at a time instead of trying to plod along a continuum of a million days. One is more manageable than the other and keeps you awake from one day to the next.

So next time a task (or life) seems too big to begin, remember the following:

* No matter how large or seemingly impossible a task, a life or a mountain might be, you only have to take one step at a time.

* When you feel yourself becoming overwhelmed and wanting to run away from making a start, just promise yourself you will do the next ten minutes and begin.

* Don't let the fearful one inside confuse and overwhelm you. Take some small action toward your goal and the fear will subside.

* Many labour intensive tasks can actually be good fun if you a. have company to help you, b. sing or listen to music while you work, and/or c. remember to keep some good chocolate by you to keep your energy up!

There is real Grace in making a start, even though you don't know quite how you will end it. If you only do things you know very well how to finish, you will only do dull things.

Notes:

60. Do you enjoy being 'cool'?

What is your view of the way of living that is currently described as being cool? Perhaps you could explain it to me?

From the outside, playing it cool appears to mean that someone might be feeling a lot about something, but they will only show a little of what they feel or indeed a little of the opposite of what they really feel to other people. Why do they do this?

It seems to be fashionable not to tell others what you love, what you hope for, when you are excited or full of pleasure in their company. I have been told that this is being 'uncool'.

I have also come to understand that playing 'hard to get' is part of playing it cool and that this is an excellent way of attracting interesting people of the opposite sex towards you. This involves feigning disinterest even though the opposite may be true.

Being hard to get is intended to make the other work harder to change your mind, even though everyone knows that everyone is interested anyway. Why else would people bother to go through the games and manoeuvres they do? Underneath all the sham is this just another insurance policy against being hurt? It seems so.

What would it be like if people were more authentic with each other and didn't try to manufacture a persona for others to see?

* What would others see if you let them?

* What do you hope they wouldn't see?

* What have you decided they shouldn't see?

* What mannerisms, expressions, behaviours or strategies have you designed to ensure that others shouldn't see you?

* Are you cool or just scared?

Unfortunately, playing it cool also obscures your sweetness, innocence, spontaneity and Grace. Most of what is left is a carefully constructed puppet, which sometimes looks 'cool' but usually just appears phoney.

Drop the act. Risk being real. Don't use up all your energy constructing another you. Live in the you that already exists. The you that exists is a work of art. Develop your appreciation and acceptance for the work of art you are.

Someone who appreciates and accepts themselves is irresistible when viewed from the outside by others and brings deep peace and Grace to the self when experienced from the inside.

Notes:

61. So you think you have a problem?

How will you solve it? Perhaps it is beginning to keep you awake at night and you are spending a good deal of time thinking about what to do?

Sometimes, it can help to become more objective and use a problem solving framework to move you forward. Apply your problem to these three stages and see what happens:

Step 1. What is happening now?
Step 2 What would you like to happen instead?
Step 3 What must be done to make the move from Step 2 to 3?

Step 1 requires you to describe the current situation you find yourself in fully. Usually this is as far as we get with our problems and is the place where we find ourselves moaning. Be objective, write down the facts and the feelings as you believe them to be. If necessary get someone you trust to help you.

Step 2 is the place where you are able to describe exactly what you want instead of what you've got. Often we don't get this far, preferring to stay stuck with our complaining.

When you have described your 'ideal scenario' fully, do a reality check. Given the resources you have: money, time, intellect, physical strength etc., can your dream be brought to fruition or is it just really a dream. (If your ideal is out of touch with reality then accepting this is part of the solution). You also need to check whether getting what you want would mean someone else being disadvantaged. Doing harm by disadvantaging others invariably bounces back to hurt you.

Then decide what is the gap in practical terms between what you've got and what you want.

Step 3 is the planning stage. If you can now clearly see what has to be done to move you from Step 1 to Step 2, break the gap down into doable tasks:

* Beside each task write what resources you have and what you lack to complete it.

* Decide who or what can help you with what you need to complete each task (buy a book, join a night class, ask a friend to support you).

* Consider how you will know when each task is complete e.g. when task a. is complete I will have written to the bank manager and followed the letter up with an appointment, or, when task b. is complete I will have weeded the front garden, planted some winter pansies and primulas. Be explicit.

* Give yourself a 'by when' date to complete each task. If you consistently break your agreements with yourself about completing things on time, you will need to examine your motivation by going back to Step 2 and checking if your 'ideal' is still what you really want. If it isn't, re-think and refine what you want instead of what you've got and start the planning steps again.

There is nothing more energy sapping than having wish lists and persistent problems going round and round in your head. Getting into practical action makes you feel better about yourself and who knows, you might just solve a problem or two while you're at it. Action purifies and if not you, then who?

Notes:

62. Give each other a different kind of feedback

Rather than give advice to your friend or partner about how they are, should be or could be, practice getting a sense of them in the moment. This sense is based on their energy or vibration and how it impacts on you, at that time, as you sit with them.

As human beings we have all been given the ability to sense others, although most of us have allowed this 'sixth sense' to fall asleep due to disuse. Instead, we have come to rely more and more heavily on the spoken word, but this method of communicating does not always take account of the more subtle information that there is to be sensed about each other.

Try this instead:

* Sit quietly with another person and close your eyes.

* Do a quick 'scan' of yourself to find out what residues of thoughts or feelings about your life or your day are within you.

* Breathe deeply and breathe out anything that prevents you from concentrating on the other person.

* When you have settled and any nervousness disappears, what feelings come to you about the other person? (These feelings might include random thoughts, tensions or sensation in the body or emotions that arise quickly and don't seem to be connected to your own state).

* You might experience sadness that you know is not yours, tiredness, giggles or an inability to relax with the other. Don't be tempted to decide what any of this means. That is not your job. Stay present.

* After 5/10 minutes, open your eyes and ask the other person whether they would like to hear about the sense of them that you have. If so, offer the information tentatively as a gift. It isn't necessary that they accept or agree with it.

All too often we value being told by experts what we are and what we should do. We rarely get straight data about ourselves without someone else's meaning or interpretation attached.

By the above means, you and your partner or friend can truly meet and give each other the gift of your attention in the moment. The more you practice, the deeper and more informing your sensing will become. Even if the other person doesn't want the feedback, you are better informed about their state and your own.

If you are part of a couple who have trouble arriving and settling together after a busy day or time apart, the above process is a respectful and loving way to reconnect.

It is a better way of settling together than the traditional gin and tonic! One way wakes you up to the other and the alcohol puts you (or some parts of you,) to sleep.

Notes:

63. What is limiting your life?

When we examine our lives and what we can have and do, we often have an invisible frame around this picture outside of which we don't go; even in our dreams.

This frame is probably made up of fears and experiences that in the past have taught us what we can't have and can't do. Some of these negatives are no longer valid and some of them are, but either way, the constricting framework we make of them limits our possibilities and our lives.

What we envision patterns our thinking and directs our action. If our vision is made smaller by what we believe we can't have or do and what we believe is impossible for us, we can only be creative in a very constricted space.

It may be easier for us to see what is inside this small space and to begin to decide how to change it or alter it around, a bit like changing your existing furniture around inside the same room. It is more difficult for us to consider a different room or different furniture because we have discounted the idea and indeed forgotten that the larger or newer possibility exists for us. We have trained ourselves not to think about what we believe we can't have.

The forgotten and invisible things that are outside our consideration for what we might have or do, set hard like concrete. We no longer try to go outside the wall we have built for ourselves and no longer remember it is there. The area inside the wall is where we live our lives; just the way things are for us.

* Do you move the same furniture around the same room of your life and call this changing?

* Think of a change you could make that would be like putting the same furniture in a new room.

* Now think of a change you could make that would be like putting new furniture in a new room.

* Now think of the reasons you habitually use for why you can't do that

Either challenge yourself, or ask a friend to challenge your reasons-why-not. Find out if they are valid or whether they are figments of the past and assumptions about the future.

Discover what makes up the frame that limits your life and step outside it in some practical way. Do or have some of the things you 'know' you can't. Once you are outside the frame you will never go back because the ways in which you delude yourself about your limitations will be exposed. Your limitations will have no role to play and no hold over you. You will be free to be creative and live on a larger scale.

Notes:

64. Living life as inquiry

Are you a person who feels most comfortable when you know all
there is to know about a situation?

Many of us are like this and it makes sense to be well informed.
Sometimes though, the process of becoming well informed is less
interesting or valuable to us than the answers we hope to gain by it.
The inquiry process is simply a means to an end.

Finding things out has become a quick and easy one step process via
the internet or reference library. You look something up, you find it,
you accept the information as true or relevant and move on to do
something else.

Obviously, certain sorts of information can be simply so or not so;
what time is the train, is there a plane from x to y, which books has
a certain author written and published? But there is other
information that is offered or accepted by us as fact, or truth that is
simply someone's opinion: a bit like the opinions you are reading
now. It may be a well or partially researched opinion but there will
be other views on the topic that are equally interesting or relevant.

The problem is that we often accept and believe too much without
reflecting or inquiring further into things. We may have our own
agenda for believing what we hear or read: it may support our own
view or opinion for example. But equally, the writer or originator of
the information may have their agenda too and this may not be
apparent to us when we are trying to formulate our own conclusions.

Become a little sceptical. Become an inquirer into what goes on in
modern life. You were given not only a memory to retain what you
read or hear, but a mind that is capable of weighing the pros and
cons of it and testing out your own conclusions; seeing where they
fit against your own experience. Collect relevant evidence to support
or disprove what you are beginning to believe, before your ideas set
like concrete in a mould.

Don't let others decide what's what on the important issues of life for you. Ask questions, be observant, decide what is going on for yourself. See where what you have discovered lines up with 'popular opinion' and where it doesn't. Find out why.

* Become curious about the things you accept and those you reject out of hand. What is threatening or meaningful to you in what you believe and what you don't?

* What is it ok for you not to know and not to understand? What are you handing over to others to decide for you when you allow this?

* Notice the acute inquisitiveness of a child or a young animal. Where and when did this sense disappear in you?

* Pep up the dullness of your senses with exotic smells, new tastes and interesting textures and sounds.

* Go and find out what you thought you already knew. No-one can do this for you and if not you, then who?

Notes:

65. Who do you agree to learn from?

Many people these days believe that learning and staying open to
new experiences is the way they want to live their lives. Fewer of us
are staying closed to new opportunities and new ways of thinking
than ever before.

Lifelong self-directed education has become common practice for
those who wish to stay awake and live a Graceful life. But we could
go further and deeper with this intention if we were less selective
about the form that education could take and who or what we would
agree to learn from.

We read self-help books (a bit like this one), we go on weekend
workshops, we spend time with teachers and gurus. We are very
choosy about who or what we will permit to change us or our view.

How would it be for you to actively seek to be taught by the
ignorant, the clumsy, the unschooled, the unattractive or the
downright commonplace? I am not suggesting that you could spend
time listening to such people in order to learn how to avoid being
like them, although you might. They have something new to offer
you.

Imbedded in everything, even the gross and the ignorant, are the
diamonds of wisdom and sense. You may have to be patient, and
allow your critical faculties to quieten, but the sweetness of truth will
be there if you persevere.

If we only allow ourselves to learn in certain ways from certain
people, we will only be able to learn certain things. The knowledge
of the things that we need to learn cannot be known to us from our
present state, which only knows what we already know. It isn't easy
to detect the absence of knowing which is presently unknown to us.
That means we can't trust our own ideas of what we should learn or
whom we should learn it from. So what can we do instead?

* Don't arrange your own learning; learn from what life puts in front
of you on a day to day basis

* Don't just learn from who or what you agree with. That is not learning, it is just shoring up your own ego

* Listen to the young, the old, the ignorant. Don't discount what they say too quickly if at all

* Actively engage in an unlearning process. Say to yourself, 'If things aren't the way I see them, how might they be instead.'.

We have open shapes in our minds rather like a child's toy. We are looking for a piece of learning of the same shape to pop itself through.   Do yourself a favour and change the shape that you recognise as education from time to time. Who knows what you will learn then.

Notes:

66. Life is like decorating a room

Sometimes life can be compared to decorating a room because the decisions we make about living and decorating can be similar.

Some people start the decorating process by moving out or protecting all the furniture; they wash down the walls and the paintwork and prepare the surfaces thoroughly for the new paint or wallpaper.

Others take short cuts, painting over whatever is below, splashing paint here and there and counting the cost in spoiled furniture afterwards. Everything will be complete in a day and they will invite friends round that evening to admire their work

Both decorating styles have their merits and their drawbacks: one is thorough and the other is quick (and probably dirty). Which would be your favourite way?

There are parallels here to the way we make changes and live our lives generally. Some people will be slow to make changes or get a project off the ground. They do their preparation first. They will research, plan and spend a long time gathering information before making any sort of move at all. Onlookers may despair that these folk will ever do anything. It could be described as 'like watching paint dry'.

Others take action first and prepare afterwards. This 'after-prep' consists of coming to conclusions about whether or not they actually like the consequences of the change they have made or the action they have taken, counting the cost and getting used to the new 'room' they have created in their lives. Sometimes there is some putting right or making amends to be done.

* When do you do your preparation; before or after you have acted?

* What would it be like to reverse your usual process?

* Not everything in life requires you to be thorough: sometimes it is more important to act quickly or you will lose your chance or 'miss the boat'.

* Some things are best done slowly and methodically, especially where the action you take will have long lasting implications for yourself or others.

* Don't get stuck with one decorating style or one way of living. Don't be continually reactive or always afraid of making a mistake. Choose how you want to respond each time you act. In order to be appropriate, your responses should be as varied as the tasks or changes you are tackling.

What is the next room in your life that requires a face-lift? What will your strategy be for tackling it? Watch yourself in action or in inaction: decide how you want to be.

What do you want to do and what speed and depth of response is needed to bring you success? Don't be habitual: change the colour of your response to life.

Notes:

67. Do you trust your own creativity?

Do you believe that you are a creative person; able to produce new ideas, new items, grow flowers, decorate your home, cook meals? Or do you think that you are an uncreative type unable to produce anything new or original?

Many times a day we are called upon to be creative and we manage it effortlessly and yet we still don't recognise this aspect of ourselves. To be creative is to be Graceful. It is the way in which we are able to mirror the great Life Force that created us.

Consider your thoughts. Every one as it arises is somehow a little different from the one before. You combine your experience, your beliefs your ideas and create a continuous stream of original thought. The components of your thought might be familiar, but each of itself is a new creation.

If you take action on a thought, that action will be a little different to every other action that you have taken before. In order to physically move to carry out the action, your body will create movements and forms that have never been done by you in this life before. They may be similar to other movements your body has made, but not the same.

Spiritually also we are in continuous ebb and flow toward and away from unity with the Source that created us.

Everything about you is a work in creation. Your brain and body produce new cells and lose old ones every minute of every day. You are never exactly the same physically or mentally from one day to the next.

So how is it then that we can fool ourselves into believing that we are always the same: ever unchanging - living an uncreative life? It may be that we have a fixed and erroneous idea of what creativity really is. Perhaps we think of friends who paint, dress-make or write and we see only differences between them and us.

Begin to think of creativity in a much wider sense:

* Remember that as your thoughts rise, your reflective process is creative

* Feel your body move: each movement you make is an original, creative dance

* Sit and feel the vibration of life running under your skin. The process of life you are engaged in is the ultimate creativity.

* Spend time considering the union that all living things share in this ultimate creativity. Think about your connection in this process and how you play your part.

Widen your sense of what true and Graceful creativity really is. Stop denying your creativity. Know yourself as an equal member in the creative process of living and take part fully.

Notes:

68. Can you let your troubles move through you?

When troubles weigh us down, the last thing we feel like doing is being active. We tend to become very sedentary, moving as little as possible and holding everything that bothers us inside.

We may be able to talk with others and share our problems; getting some good advice from friends and trusted ones in the process. This doesn't always seem to bring us the increased energy and the lightness we need to get on and move past whatever is our trouble.

Sadness and negativity seem to find a home in our joints and the spaces between our organs. Sometimes we can even feel ourselves aching with the burden of having 'our stuff' stuck in the nooks and crannies of our bodies. The next time this happens to you, try doing the reverse of your inclinations and attempt to move and shift your mood through you and out.

* Look through your music selection and find melodies with different beats to support this cleaning out process. You will need slow, soulful music, pop or other music with a definite up-beat, wild world or clubbing sounds in a variety of speeds and some music to meditate to. Consider your current state of bodily fitness and keep your movements within the range of what is comfortable and safe for you.

* Clear as big a space as possible in your room. Light candles in safe places and get some water to drink. Put on loose, comfortable clothing and have a blanket or shawl to put on and take off as you heat up and cool down. Make sure you won't be disturbed for at least an hour.

* Start with the slow soulful music and begin to stretch out your muscles – don't leave any part of you out until you are relaxed and warm. (You should spend at least 10 minutes doing this warm up) Then move around your room in whatever way pleases you, to this gentle feminine music.

* When your body begins to feel as if it wants to move a little faster (and not before) change the music to something with more of a beat. Line your breathing up with the beat and become more energetic in your movements. Up the anti inside yourself and feel how strong and assertive you can be as your body moves. You should begin to feel quite hot and also a little impatient with the repetitive movements that the beat of the music demands of you. Make sure you take sips of water frequently.

* Change the music to something wilder and more energetic. Within the confines of your fitness and ability, lose the regular beat and give way to the surges of the music as it passes through you. Relax yourself (especially your jaw) and really go for it until you can move no more. At this stage, change the music to something similar but slower so you can begin to cool down and gather yourself once again. By this time you should be sweating profusely. Don't be surprised at the emotions that race through you – laughing, crying, raging, longing. Let them all come and let them all go. Make any sounds that come whenever you feel prompted.

* Wrap yourself in your blanket and drop to the floor. Sit with your candle and experience your emptiness and calmness and the absence of negativity.

* When you begin to grow chilly and before your limbs stiffen, stretch out again gently and run yourself a hot bath.

Talking and thinking are not the only processes we have at our disposal to lessen the load of the trouble we feel. Since the most ancient times our ancestors have used music, drumming and movements to invoke different moods.

If this works for you, why not join a regular class where Gabrielle Roth's 5 rhythm dancing or something similar is practiced.

Don't sit there 'til you 'set': move it!

Notes:

69. Are you a starter or a finisher?

Lots of us have a strong preference for either starting things or finishing them. Unless we know which we are, we can become very puzzled about our waxing and waning motivations to get the things done that we want to do.

Do you have lots of good ideas, many sudden enthusiasms, and enjoy starting up new things? Are there lots of unfinished projects lying around that you know you must finish one day, but not today?

Do you feel you lack creativity, can't always figure out how you want to do something but often enjoy finishing things off that others have started? Brand new ideas don't always come readily to you, but you always know exactly how to provide the detail to make someone else's brainwave work.

These two styles, or ways of doing things, need the services of the other to bring things into being and to a successful conclusion, but people who are starters and those who are finishers don't always appreciate each other and cooperate.

Starters are often highly conceptual and have become appreciated and applauded for this ability. They can sometimes become inclined to look 'down' upon finishers as people without the creative spark, forgetting that they need them if any of their ideas are to work in everyday life.

Finishers are usually pragmatic, methodical people who pride themselves on doing a good job and getting things done. They may believe that starters are full of 'airy-fairy' ideas and lack practical common sense that is of use in the world.

In order for a finisher to help a starter they will need to understand what an idea is meant to achieve, who is supposed to benefit from it etc. For a starter to help a finisher they will need a clear view of how much time or money is available to complete the project.

Ideally each 'style' needs to learn some of the skills of the other:

* Starters could learn to prepare a project plan, how to follow its steps and how to remain within time and money constraints. They need to hold the practical purpose for which they are creating something in mind and not be distracted into the realms of the fantastic at others' expense.

* Starters often need to learn how to gain the support of others to help them do practical things.

* Starters should use discipline to prevent themselves starting something new before the project before is completed, (by themselves or someone else)

* Finishers could practice brainstorming and visualisation techniques to awaken their latent creativity

* Finishers should not become so lost in the detail of doing something that they forget the original idea and what it is for

* Finishers should balance their idea of perfection with the idea of utility. Asking the question 'is this fit for purpose and is it good enough now?', can be useful.

* Before blaming starters for not appearing to appreciate their skills, finishers should make sure that they appreciate themselves.

Ideas people (starters) and craftsmen and women (finishers) have been at loggerheads down through the ages. It really is time that we all learnt to appreciate the fit and necessity between our different ways of doing things.

Notes:

70. Making up our minds about how things will be

Do you decide how things are likely to be, what people might say or how an event is bound to turn out?

When we do this, we close down the parts of ourselves that are capable of being surprised by something new. Instead we open the parts of ourselves that are programmed to recognise and respond only to this and not that: not that or not that either.

This means that however things or people turn out to be, we will only see what we expect to see or recognise as lining up with our self-programming. Anything other than that which meets our expectations about how things are, will be discounted or ignored as we busily search for that we were sure would happen.

Whatever people say to us, if we have already decided what they mean, that is what we will hear. Alternatively, we will hear what they actually say, but decide that they mean what we have previously decided they would.

What a dull little world we create in order to avoid the opportunity of being surprised and seduced by the unfamiliar. What do you think is the worst that can happen if something brand new and totally unexpected happens to you?

* Are you afraid of not knowing what to do or say?

* Do you worry that you won't be able to cope?

* Do you believe that it's far better to be right and to know, than to be taken by surprise?

* Are you afraid of appearing foolish or inept?

Whatever your fear of just staying in the present and allowing things and people to happen to you, nothing is worse than the dreariness and dryness of permanent control and death by-working-it-all-out-beforehand!

No matter how much you know about everything, there is nothing that can prepare you for the miraculous wonder and Grace-of-being that comes with standing vulnerably before the unknown.

It will happen to us all one day when you stand before the greatest of all unknowns. Why not take the opportunity to get used to it now while you live?

Arguably we are here to learn to live fully in the present and to learn to die well. Stop trying to insure yourself against the Great Surprise: just let it have you.

Notes:

71. The Collusion of Couples

Viewed from the outside, the relationships of couples we know often appear inexplicable. It can be difficult to see why some couples remain together. They may even appear to wish to part and move on if they are unhappy, but quite often this just doesn't happen.

What is it that they are playing out together that keeps them in situ, rather than parting and living a more fulfilling life?

Viewed from the inside, we may be aware that our relationship with our partner is not perfect. Sometimes we feel that he or she is unreasonable, unkind or doesn't love us the way we are. We may find it hard to like this person that we remain with year after year. So why do we?

Although couples may not be content in their relationships, they often have an unspoken agreement to shore it up, keep it going, and put up with demanding or unreasonable behaviours as they do so.

Although what is happening in the relationship at present is uncomfortable for a couple, it may seem better than stopping what is going on or changing the behaviour in a more positive way. This is because whatever is happening has been set up by a series of unspoken agreements over time to keep things the way they are. These agreements have become part of the foundations of the relationship.

Why should someone put up with what appears to be an abusive relationship with a partner? Because, unlikely as it seems, there will be a payoff that makes it all worth it. What could such a payoff be? To stay weak or dependent, to stay with a pattern of behaviour that is familiar, to enjoy making up: in short to stay with the known which provides both people with security.

What could happen if the abuser attends to his or her behaviour and 'reforms'? The colluding agreement is broken and the relationship can fall apart. The role played by each partner has to change, when one of them changes. For every persecutor, someone has to play victim. If that person drops that role, the relationship alters radically and sometimes the partners can no longer find a reason to be together.

Why should someone accept that their partner is unfaithful? Because no matter how difficult, the payoff may be worth it: less pressure and resentment about having to have unwanted sex, grateful behaviour from the unfaithful one arising from guilt, more security around the raising of children.

If the unfaithful partner ends the affair, he or she might have to face up to and attempt to do something about whatever is lacking at home and things might become less balanced and peaceful there as a result. Both partners would have to communicate openly and honestly about their needs and the possibility of getting them met within the 'marriage', with the risk that the relationship might not survive. Sometimes the 'vitamin supplement' of a lover is less disruptive than having the relationship catch a cold!

We all have unspoken agreements in our long term relationships. Some of them are necessary to provide the cement between the building blocks of our lives with a partner.

Every once in a while it's important to review your agreements and contracts with your partner (unspoken or otherwise). How are they serving the relationship? Is it time to change the way you lean on each other emotionally?

* What habits have you fallen into to keep the peace? Do these habits work in a positive way or do they mean that one or both of you are colluding to keep things the same?

* Which one's behaviour appears to be most disruptive or destructive of the relationship when viewed from the outside? With insider knowledge, which one of you is it really?

* How might you grow or change if you weren't in a relationship with this person? Why can't you do that now?

* What's in it for you to keep these games and collusions going?

* What might happen if you didn't?

A relationship is a bit like a car which is expected to keep going, mile after mile, without a service.

Make time to service your relationship before it breaks down. If you aren't confident that you can be positive and impartial, get skilful and trustworthy help. Nothing keeps going for ever without attention. Give your relationship a spring clean and feel the benefit!

Notes:

72. Keeping control of your relationship

Who keeps control of your relationship? Who is in charge? How do you know if someone is trying to take the lead; to make things go his or her way?

There are two clear control mechanisms that alert a couple to which one of them is trying to take charge of the relationship and when: sex and money. How a couple manage these important issues, tells a lot about the health of the partnership.

* Do you each keep your own money, not sharing or letting the other one know about what you spend and when?

* Is one of you the wage earner and do you give the other 'pocket money' or 'housekeeping', rather than share what you have?

* Do you withhold money from your partner when you are angry with them?

* Do you spend money on yourself to compensate when your relationship is not going well?

* Do you refuse to make love to your partner frequently or have you stopped making love altogether?

* When you make love is it quick or perfunctory; designed to give you an orgasm and nothing more?

* Do you lie there like a piece of wood and refuse to hold or please your partner when you have sex?

* Do you promise that you will make love tonight, tomorrow or next week and then make an excuse not to do so?

All the above are tactics that give one partner power over the other and spring from a desire to have control, sometimes because that person is angry.

You may argue that there are perfectly good reasons for a partner to withhold sex from the other. Sometimes there are, but there should be no good reason not to cuddle or hold your partner and let them know that they are loved, even if making love is not possible temporarily. If you don't love them of course, this may not be possible. The question then is, 'What are you doing together', and the answer would be 'making each other miserable'.

If one person tends to over spend, then it is a good idea for some sort of helpful agreement to prevent this, to be made between the two people. But this agreement might be of the sort where two signatures are required on a cheque, rather than one partner only having access to the couple's finances. Resources should be shared and no adult should be given pocket money as if they were a child.

Do a health check on your relationship. If power and control behaviours are happening, see if you can get to the underlying issue and sort it out before it's too late.

Even if other areas of the relationship appear to be going well, control issues will eventually wreck what you have. Bring your partnership to a more mature position; each person must take responsibility for helping the relationship to grow up.

Notes:

73. Colour yourself happier on the cold days

Are you one of those people who dread the dark of winter, especially after Christmas?
Do you find yourself going to bed earlier and earlier, attempting to hibernate the winter away?

Here are some suggestions that may help you make it cheerfully through to the spring again:

* Pay attention to the colour of the rooms you usually sit it at home

* Buy some daylight bulbs or a light box

* Wear brighter and more vibrant clothing

* If possible, have your annual holiday in the winter rather than (or if you're able, in addition to) the summer

Bland or dark decorations at home will not help to keep you cheerful and awake. If you follow current trends for painting everything white or cream, you may be surprised to know that the neutrality of these decors may not be helpful to you.

Try painting your room yellow, pink, orange, turquoise or lime green. These colours are uplifting and awakening. They are also fun and will make you smile. Create summer indoors. A few tins of paint are not expensive and can radically change the look of your home in a day or two. Ask someone else to help you and/or paint to music.

Buy or borrow a light box or some special 'daylight' bulbs. Sit in front of these for at least an hour every day. (I always turn mine on when I'm writing these Gracenotes). Take your light box to work with you and put it on your desk if appropriate.

Have you noticed how we get out our dark clothing in the winter, reserving beautifully coloured garments for the summer? We probably needed to do this when the fabrics that winter clothes were made from had to be dry cleaned and couldn't be washed..

Wear something bright and beautiful every day, even if it is only a scarf or a tie. The vibration of a clear, bright colour will lift your mood (and everyone else's).

If you can, have a holiday at the end of January or beginning of February. These often feel like the darkest times of year and if you can afford to travel to the sun and the clear light at this time you will give yourself and your body a real boost.

Take care of your general health: eat fruit and green leafy vegetables when you can. Take exercise with others at least one evening a week. Don't sit in front of the television as soon as it gets dark.

It makes sense to do everything you can to stop dreading the winter. If you don't you will spend more than half your life in dread. That's not much fun is it?

Notes:

74. Between one place and another isn't nowhere

Most of us will agree that change is a positive thing. This agreement usually refers to the sort of change that is about stopping one thing and starting another. However, most significant changes that human beings will experience in their lives cannot be described in those simplistic terms.

In all change, we stop doing or being something, but when such change is complex or life changing, the transitional place we go to or become next has little connection with starting to do or being something new.

The place we begin to occupy may seem characterless or empty and make us doubt that we will ever again know who we are or what we are supposed to do next. This emptiness could be considered to be a 'void', an apparently nothing place where we know we aren't what we were, but don't yet know what or how to be instead.

Because of our mistaken belief that positivity and leading a cheery productive life full of direction and achievement is paramount, we may do anything we can to escape from the void. We thereby miss the opportunity for true change and growth. For the void is a natural, and despite how it feels when we are in it, useful stage in the process of change. Without it, we cannot truly begin to evolve into what we are to become and will only be able to manifest change at a fragile, cosmetic level.

The void, through its loneliness and lack of knowing, teaches who we are and what we are capable of being. As a result of separation, divorce, ill health, an accident, retirement, moving from childhood to adolescence, losing your job, moving to a new area, we learn many new things about ourselves that change us forever. It takes time though to integrate what we have learnt and to become those changes fully.

If, when a relationship finishes, we rush around looking for a new partner immediately, what we have learnt from the old relationship is lost rather than integrated. That often means that we have to learn those lessons all over again sometimes at the expense of the new relationship, rather than moving on.

If when we retire, we quickly join clubs, go on outings, take holidays; anything to fill the time, we won't be able to integrate this new stage of our lives and to come to terms with the fact that our career as it was has now ended. Better to be still and quiet for a while as our new situation makes itself fully felt in us.

* Being between one thing and another is not being nowhere. It is a relevant and vital stage of the process of change for human beings.

* After a personal tragedy or bereavement, resist being 'brought back to life' by well meaning friends. Choose to spend time with quieter people who will understand that you are engaged in the important personal work of integrating your changed circumstances into your view of your world.

* Guard your transition times. Let them take as long as they take. Don't be rushed out of them by people who believe that it is healthy to be always doing or saying something.

Notes:

75. We may have left, but we are still there

When the delight goes out of a relationship, a project or a situation, there are several different options open to us:

* We can leave

* We can attempt to regain the delight by working and changing the situation

* We can leave and yet remain where we are

The first two, although difficult, are simple enough to carry out. The third, although apparently easy, is the least satisfying for us in the long term.

When we are fully engaged in a partnership, a project or a job, we bring our emotions and our energy to it as an investment: this, together with our physical presence is our part in a bargain of involvement. When things go wrong and we experience disappointment and a wish to leave, we begin to take back our investment of energy and emotion before we physically leave the situation.

This taking back of part of ourselves is a necessary stage in removing ourselves from where we've been. For some people, however, this stage can take a very long time and becomes a way of life, rather than part of the process that will eventually bring complete separation.

The withdrawing of our energy and emotion from someone or something that we have invested deeply in, is inevitable as we firstly become disenchanted and see things (perhaps for the first time) as they are and then begin to disassociate ourselves from what we no longer love.

Ideally, our bodies then follow the pattern of separation that our emotions and energies have already taken by leaving. We often feel that this is impossible, especially when there are issues of duty, care, hurting others, fear of not being able to get 'a better one', losing out financially etc. These fears may be true and valid, but they are also excuses for subjecting ourselves and others to a situation based on convenience rather than truth and love.

* If you feel that your emotions and energies are no longer associated with a situation you are in, be honest with others involved. See if anything can be done to bring something alive back to the agreement.

* If your body just keeps turning up, but the rest of you is elsewhere, decide whether you will go or stay, but don't try to do both. When you do this you are short changing yourself and others.

* Don't kid yourself that you are being kind by staying with someone or something when energetically you have left. A clean break may be initially painful for all concerned, but it would at least give the other the possibility of eventually being with someone who can be with them 100%. It might also give you back your life all in one body, all in one place.

Notes:

76. Understanding your power

Perhaps you don't see yourself as a powerful person. You may feel that your boss is, or your teachers were, but you aren't. That may be because you don't really understand the nature of power.

Are you thinking of power as something that one person has over another: the parent over the small child, the bully over her victim?

Power, in its truest sense is something that is shared with others, not something used to get one over on someone else. If you have to force someone to do something, that is a sign of your disempowered state, not your power. In order to be truly powerful, you have to give up the desire to make others do things and be alongside them instead, sharing the ability to get things done.

The more awake you are, the less force you will use to get your own way. The truly Graceful individual has the power to get buy-in from others without coercing them. Why is this?

* A truly powerful person is sometimes vulnerable; sharing difficulties and weaknesses without attempting to hide them. They don't put on a tough act.

* A truly powerful person recognises the worth of all human beings as equal, even if their levels of skill or positions/situations are different. They treat people with respect.

* A truly powerful person is clear about what they want and who they are. They don't manipulate.

* A truly powerful person is consistent emotionally; people know where they are with him or her. They are trusted.

Rethink your ideas about power. Notice how you use yours. Think about the a toddler having an ear splitting tantrum in a public place because it wants an ice cream, a bigger child taking a toy from a smaller one, an adolescent with a blaring radio on the beach, a young woman flirting with another man because she knows her partner is watching, or a father screaming at his child. These are all ways of using power over others.

Consider a facilitator supporting a group as they work through an issue, a manager coaching a member of staff through a new procedure, parents allowing teenagers to negotiate ground rules for behaviour, lovers giving each other choices in their relationship. These are ways of using power **with** others.

You use power with, rather than over others when you know in your heart you are strong, centred, loving and loved. Once you recognise the source of your own power, which is the greatest and most creative Source of all, you have no need to bully, harass, force or make anyone do anything. Most of the time, people will be more than willing to help you do what is needed, because they know that you will help them in their turn.

What goes around comes around. If you force, coerce, manipulate and treat others as objects by imposing your power and will on them, they will find a way to become what you make them, and they will retaliate. Or someone else will in their stead.

You set in motion a train of aggression when you begin to use your power over others. This way of behaving is born out of your fear that you are weak. Better to examine this fear and work with it, than to continue imposing it on others in the form of misused power.

Notes:

77. Are you the angry one?

Are you a person that tends to express anger quicker and more readily than any other emotion. Are you the first to spot a supposed injustice, the noisiest in defence of yourself and are you well known for giving your loved ones a hard time when things appear to go against your wishes.

Anger is an emotion that can rise quickly; sometimes so quickly that it appears to be out of our control. It can be all absorbing and take up all our energy until it subsides. It is an excellent way to mask what is really going on inside us because we aren't able to attend to more subtle feelings while we are in the grip of our anger.

If we were able to slow the swift rise of our anger, we would notice something softer and sadder going on beneath it. We might find fear, sadness and a great desire for connection. Do you think that this might be going on for you?

* Notice the people or events that trigger your anger. There will be something about these people or things that you care about deeply. What is it you really want from them?

* When your anger subsides, can you catch traces of another emotion left behind? It might be sadness or fear.

* Have you noticed that you can become most angry most often with the people you love most? Why should this be?

We experience a great desire for connection with those we love most. As children, when those that cared for us appeared to disagree with what we did or what we wanted, we would become afraid of losing the loving connection with them that we needed. This hopeful vulnerability and desire to be loved by our dear ones stays with us as we grow to adulthood. The fear that was created in us as children around the loss of love does too.

As we grew and our vulnerability became unacceptable to us, we learnt to cover our fear of disconnection from what and who we love with anger. Our loved ones and friends are likely to be puzzled and hurt by what seems to them to be continued aggressive over-reactions. Sadly, the furious outbursts that are triggered by our fear are likely to result in the disconnection we most hope to avoid as others withdraw from us and our anger.

* Become observant about your trigger points. Notice the physical changes in your body as anger starts to rise: increased breathing and heart rate, tightness across the diaphragm and belly.

* Try to put a gap between your anger rising and the communication of your feelings to others. Take time to breathe, slow down and notice the feelings beneath the feelings.

* Think kindly of yourself. Somewhere inside you there is fear. Remember what you want most is to be loved. You are a loving person.

* Try not to take what is said to you by others personally. Most of what they say, most of the time, is about them, not you.

* Others can dislike your behaviour or disagree with your ideas and still love and care for you at the same time.

* If you can, begin to write down the thoughts and the feelings you experience when you are angry. When you are calm, read what you have written. See if you can spot the vulnerability under the anger.

* Attempt to communicate from the part of you that wants connection with the other, not the angry part that is trying to hide everything else.

The vulnerable, loving one is the part of you that is having the courage to show its true nature. Angry one is the camouflager, attempting to protect the tender feelings of the young child. Angry one has served you well in the past, but you no longer need its

protection. Loving one is the real and Graceful you now. It is time to let this one have its rightful position in your life and your relationships.
Let the shield of anger drop. The battle is already won and you haven't noticed

Notes:

78. Big Fish Little Pond?

Can you remember when you were a child, changing from your first infant classes at school to the next level up where everything was so much bigger and you felt so much smaller.

When you left school, college or university and began your working life, you may have felt rather adrift amongst so many people. Starting at the bottom of the ladder felt different to being at the top of your particular educational system. You had moved from a little pond to a much bigger one and proportionally had become a much smaller fish.

For some people, these sorts of proportional shifts to a larger arena can be comfortable and welcome. They enjoy the impersonal feel of being one of many others. There are many places to hide from the spotlight of attention and they can get on with what they have to do. They are at liberty to observe and reflect on the diversity of people and things swimming around with them in their big pond. Such individuals may almost try to merge into the crowd, enjoying the freedom from exposure that this gives them.

For others, the loss of attention and the feeling of being less important as an individual amongst so many others is not comfortable. They may complain about the size of the group of people they find themselves in, saying that they feel lost and unable to get themselves heard amongst all the others. If they have been known for a particular skill or attribute elsewhere, they may try to wear this previous reputation as a label in the new situation. By this means they hope to make themselves known as 'someone' rather than the newness and anonymity of being one of many.

Which size pond do you prefer and how big or small a fish do you wish to be?

* Do you prefer to be a small fish whilst you are settling into a new situation? This gives you the chance to arrive without drawing attention to yourself until you find out how things are.

* When you join a group of people talking in a social situation, do you enter quietly, listening until you catch the drift of the conversation or do you come in with a bang, deliberately drawing attention to yourself and your arrival?

* Do you like to make your mark quickly, not waiting too long to influence your situation?

* How much information do you need to gather before you feel productive or are able to contribute your views in a new job, a conversation or a relationship?

* Do you sometimes involve yourself too soon, before you know the facts and eventually have cause to regret it?

Whether you prefer to be a big or small fish in a small or big pond doesn't really matter. What does have more significance is whether you have the choice to change your style and your preferences or remain stuck in one way mode for ever.

* Identify your style and watch yourself swimming in the ponds of your choice.

* Watch others with a different style. (You may find that these are people that you aren't immediately drawn to and find them either too attention seeking, or to much part of the wallpaper).

* Every now and again, speak or act as they would. See what reaction you get and what it feels like.

* Incorporate a few 'different size fish' behaviours into your life.

We all have much to learn from others. Often we learn the most interesting things from people whose behaviour irritates us. Have a bit more fun in your pond. If not you, then who?

Notes:

79. Doubting Thomas.....bye, bye.

Are you a 'doubting Thomas? Are you a sceptic? It **is** wise to be cautious isn't it? There are so many people trying to 'get you' aren't there?

How do you know this? You read the newspapers: watch the news on television. Unscrupulous people are everywhere, you say, so you are justified in your doubt and your caution.

Let's examine the case you are making for doubt. Think carefully of the possible cost of 'coming unstuck', being 'taken for a ride', becoming the victim of a liar, a fraudster, a conman or woman. I see the basis of your argument.

But there is another way to consider the argument and it goes like this: what is the true cost of keeping yourself, your belongings and concerns confined, locked away, stored in safekeeping? If you doubt your ability to be safe enough in the world, how can you live fully in it?

You have a point because yes, sometimes bad things do happen to good people.   But think carefully: what happens to doubting, sceptical, stay-at-home or lock-it-all-away and keep-it-safe people?

Nothing happens and how interesting is that?

And what happens to don't-let-anyone-in, don't-let-yourself-out people.

Nothing and no-one happens. Nothing comes in and nothing goes out and how isolating and lonely is that?

The true cost of a defending-against, protecting-from and doubting life is a small, tight, self constructed prison of scepticism and doubt. What can this lead to but a virtual, unlived life.

Are you too doubting of life to live it in a bigger way? Is your small cell enough for you? What a painful way to guard yourself from things that may never happen anyway and in the event that they do, you could choose to learn, recover and move on.

How long will you keep this up? Until your life ends and your doubting with it? If your answer is **NO** to a life lived doubtfully, when and how will you swop this for something new – today, tomorrow, next year?

You can change it in an instant. Allow your thinking to expand and follow these steps if you wish to be free:

1.Realise that your doubt isn't a reason not to live life and do things, but is an indication of **why** you don't want to take part: it is simply information about the nature of your fear. It is teaching you about yourself.

2.Understand that if you don't take part in living, you won't be able to take part in your own life's direction and growth: something/someone else will do that for or to you.

3.See it as gardeners do. Anything living that is not growing is probably dying. Make your choice now.

4.Accept that everything you are trying to keep safe and protect (whether it is your heart, your home, your car, your reputation, those you love) will one day have to be left behind when you leave life.

5.Therefore, make a decision about whether to continue to put all that doubting, defending energy into protecting what you have, or whether to stop now while you have free choice.

Is it really worth the risk of never taking a risk?

Even in the worst case you may find that losing things and people, although painful at the time, opens you to a more courageous life full of greater possibility.

Be prepared to love it and/or lose it (whatever it is) without doubting and protecting. Then you may not have to.

So say it now and mean it: 'bye, bye Doubting Thomas'. If not now, then when?

Notes:

80. Do you fall in and out of love?

When we fall in love, we believe we have met the most marvellous, magical human being ever. But before too long we may begin to notice that they aren't so perfect after all.

'Why did they hide their real character from me?', you wonder. ' I would never have fallen in love with this person if I had been able to see what they were really like,'.

At that stage many relationships end, the participants feel that they have become older and wiser and they part. Often when they meet a new partner, they will make exactly the same or similar mistakes all over again; believing they have found perfection, gradually becoming disillusioned and believing they have been duped.

We put the blame for the disillusionment firmly on the other person, repeatedly refusing to see that we have projected our desire for perfection onto them. When subsequently we take our projections back, as we must over time, the truth reveals them as they always were. Sometimes both people do this simultaneously, leaving two puzzled and disappointed people who have both been expelled from fairyland.

At this stage, and not before, it is possible to start the painstaking work of building a relationship based on reality, rather than one based on illusions of perfection in the other. Unfortunately, many couples feel too shocked, hurt or angry to do this. It is easier to part and fall in love with another perfect person and on and on they go. 'Why does this always happen to me?' we hear such people say. If only they could see that this falling in and out of love scenario is not done to them, but is something they bring to themselves.

There is nothing wrong with falling in love: it is one of the most exhilarating feelings in the world. It has its limitations though, as it

172

isn't based on reality and won't last long in the cold light of everyday living.

Are you idealistic and romantic?   Do you project fanciful notions of perfection on your partner? Do you blame them when you begin to see the truth of what and who they are?

* Now is the time to begin the work of being a part of a couple.

* Stop projecting your ideas of what is perfect onto them and begin to see the truth of what they are.

* Stop judging what they really are as lacking: stop putting your attention on what you don't like about them.

* Begin to appreciate their sweetness and tell them. What you put your attention on grows.

Grow up: begin to appreciate the reality of what you have in the other. Be who you really are and allow your partner to do the same. If you feel compelled to change something, change the wallpaper. Love your partner as they are and if you can't, leave them. Take responsibility for being mistaken; don't blame them.

Notes:

81. Do you have an impossible task oppressing you?

Is your office so cluttered you can't see your desk? Is your living room so badly in need of a lick of paint that you don't want to sit there? Is the garden so overgrown that you are sure it would take weeks to put right?

When we have these seemingly impossible situations in our lives and environments, the weight of knowing that they are there, unsorted, undone and out of control, is at the back of our minds all the time, even when we are enjoying ourselves with something else.

Things that need doing but that we don't do, don't go away, nor do we start work on clearing them up because there seems an overwhelming amount to do to put things right. At the same time we blame ourselves for not at least making the effort.

Try this:

* Don't think about the job as a whole, just work for an hour and after this time stop if you want to.

* Don't be in too much of a hurry to finish. It's been there for quite some time, so why rush to get it all done now?   Be peaceful and methodical: go slowly.

* Get up early and do your hour before the normal start of your day. Don't leave it until evening, when the pressure to be doing something else has grown too large and you are too tired.

* Get the job in order and do first things first. Work through systematically, an hour at a time. Don't do a bit here and a bit there in a random way, or you won't see the benefit of your labours.

* Notice the pressure easing as you do the job little by little. Enjoy this sensation.

* Unclutter as you go. Keep a large supply of refuse bags and throw things away or recycle that you haven't used for some time. Tie the bags and don't go back to them. Put them out to be taken by refuse/recycling collectors regularly.

*Clean as you go. As each stage of the job is finished, clean the space and leave it fresh to return to tomorrow.

Somewhere along the line, you will notice that you have done more than there is to do and working on the job will have become a habit. You will struggle less with not wanting to do it and may even find that you are enjoying yourself.

Don't be tempted to give up because things are starting to look so much better. Don't spoil your new reputation as 'she/he who gets things done' by quitting too soon.

Make sure you take time to enjoy what you have done. Really appreciate your efforts and rethink your ideas about what you are willing to achieve. Give yourself a treat and wait a week or two before you start the next 'impossible' job.

Notes:

82. Living Generously

We all have times when we do something generous: pay more than we intended because we saw the perfect present for someone, drop money into a collecting box, write a cheque so someone else can have what they need. We give of what we have with a kind intention. Sometimes though we give because we think we should. The gift is given out of a sense of duty or guilt and without the generosity of heart that accompanies giving freely.

Living generously is not so much a series of acts of giving in response to a prompting outside ourselves. True generosity is more embedded as a way of life. What would you expect to do and feel if you were living generously:

* grateful for your life and what you have whether that is judged as a little or a lot

* a responsiveness to what is needed, for yourself or others. Being quick to spot what is lacking and providing it when possible

* the living of a simple life in terms of possessions: having enough to meet your needs and not too much more

* giving freely what is needed for others: not making a grand gesture about the act of giving. Doing this anonymously when possible.

* often giving your time rather than giving things

* being generous to yourself; treating yourself because you believe you are deserving

* taking care of anything living because you feel the responsibility of connection

So you can see that living generously is an ongoing way of life, stemming from the belief that all beings are interconnected and giving to one is being generous to all.

Sadly, the opposite way of living is often evident in our society. What is that like: we believe mostly in meeting our needs or the needs of our immediate family. We act as if we are in some great competition where the prize is getting enough for us at the expense of others. Life is often mean in modern society. People behave as if there isn't enough to go around and of course, when they do this, there isn't.

We are mean when we worry about where the next this and that is coming from. Mostly, it all works out in the end, but instead of trusting generously, we live life as if we won't get enough air to breathe.

Meanness works like a spell on living beings. It shows on the outside and in the sort of life we lead. We hoard, we use just a little, eking out what we have, we are afraid someone will steal from us.

Life will steal our time from us, if we don't give it away first. Live a big, fat, generous life.

Notes:

83. Metamorph between here and there

What does a journey mean to you?

Is it the time you spend between leaving somewhere and arriving somewhere else? Do you like to travel comfortably but wish to get where you are going next as soon as possible?

When you think this way, you miss the opportunity, already foreshortened by high speed travel, to become a different person, belonging nowhere except in the transitional place that travel is.

In bygone days people were born, grew up, got married and died during journeys they took from one place to another. Today we can be from one side of the globe to another in 24 hours or less.

The time in an airport is impatiently spent waiting to board an aircraft. The time in an aircraft is impatiently spent waiting to land at an airport. The journey is rarely appreciated as anything other than something to be got through: a means to an end.

* Do you do this?

* Do you treat your life in this way too?

On long haul flights, there is the unreality of slipping over time lines and gaining and losing hours (none of which really exist unless you agree to it). If you want, this could set the scene for you to become whoever you wish for the duration of your journey and who knows how far beyond.

After all, you are neither here nor there (a bit like that mysterious time between the money leaving your bank account and arriving in someone else's) You are not where or who you were and not yet what or where you will be when you arrive.

* So who are you as you hurtle through the sky?

You have the opportunity to change - ideas, opinions, habits, defences or delusions – before you arrive. You could read something you never would, meet people you never could, wear something you never should. On the other hand you could watch a video movie, eat a few plastic meals and moan. The choice is yours.

However many delays or inconveniences you encounter on your journey, travelling is still an exotic and amazing experience if you allow it to be: an initiation or preparation for what is to come when you arrive.

Consider: air or rail travel could well be a complete illusion. We get into a metal tube at one end and get out at another. Who says we go anywhere? Think about it and give your mind a stretch.

Don't take so much for granted. When you travel you are taking part in a miracle. Where is the Grace in becoming so bland, nondescript and acceptant as travellers that we allow ourselves to be herded like half asleep sheep around the globe.

Wake up: every molecule in your body is being thrust through the heavens. How can you possibly believe that you will arrive exactly the same as you departed?

* How would you like to be different when you arrive?

Spend your journey time well. Make notes, write poetry, take photographs, accost strangers, wear fancy dress, eat only fruit. Most of all hope to meet and begin to know yourself without recognition.

Notes:

84. Are you a bully, a victim or both?

Most of us would be horrified if we were labelled as a bully. We see in our minds pictures of school playgrounds with weaker children being tormented by physically overbearing boys or girls. As adults we have more choices than children have but don't always take them.

Many people, who know in their hearts that they use coercive power over others in their adult lives, also have memories of being bullied as small children by adults or at school. Such people can usually tell the tale of the time when they began to retaliate with force and see that as the moment after which they were never bullied again.

Although we have come to consider the bully and the victim as completely different character types, with little in common that we can see, they are inextricably linked together in life's great dance of survival.

If there were no bullies in the world, there would be no victims. If as adults not one of us were in some way willing to take on the role of victim, it would not be possible for anyone to act the bully.

We can consider bullying as an attacking role and being a victim as a defensive one, but this need not necessarily be so. Many people, particularly in partnerships, use the victim stance as an attacking one:.......

* 'Look what you've done to me.'

* ' See how unhappy you've made me.'

.....are ways of verbalising that tendency to attack back in a victim. Conversely, bullying is often used as a defence: a way of keeping safe and keeping control.....

* ' You will do as I ask or I can't stay here.'

* ' I'm not putting up with that. Do it my way or you'll be sorry.'

It's also quite common for a bully and a victim to change places when things aren't going their way. The bully to victim switch can sound like this......

* ' Well what can I do but shout when you will never listen to me otherwise.'

* ' I had to push you because I just couldn't take your nagging any more: you do my head in when you go on and on: you made me do it.'

When the victim switches to bullying, you might hear things like this.....

* 'You've made me miserable for years and now it's your turn. You'll just have to put up with it.'

* 'The doctor says your behaviour has made me ill. Now I have to take antidepressants that lower my sex drive so we won't be making love any more. It's your fault, not mine.

Being a bully and being a victim are not completely different ways of meeting the world. They are at different ends of the same spectrum of behaviour and they are both fear based. It may look as if the victim is the fearful one, but the bully's main rationale for his/her behaviour is to hide their own fear, vulnerability and inadequacy from the other. The victim has found strength in their apparent weakness by being able to control the bully's tendency to bully and in the righteousness of their situation.

The bully may appear to be the one aggressing the other, but the adult victim's entrenched position of 'poor little me' is often a piece of drama designed to raise bullying behaviours in the other. The bully then feels shame and guilt. The payoff for the victim is that they can feel done to and the innocent party. But the truth is quite different to the way it looks at first sight.

We all have something of the bully and the victim in us. Have some compassion for the part of you that feels it has to take part in the drama. Bringing the game into the light of full awareness will return us to our innocence and a more Graceful state of being.

Notes:

85. Everyone wants a little piece (or is it peace?).

Last evening, the phone rang ten times and I let the calls go on answer phone after 9pm. (There just has to be a part of the day for me).

All the callers except one wanted something and I began to feel as if I needed to be bigger, fatter and generally more substantial so there would be more to go round.

Do you know that feeling? There is just not enough of you to go round? We dream of a time when we are alone and unpestered: no commitments, dates nor obligations – no need to feel guilty for not delivering to someone, somewhere.

It sounds wonderful doesn't it. But how long would the wonder last: a week, two weeks, forever?

If no-one wanted anything from us, what would that feel like? Imagine it now:

* Sitting alone in your home

* The phone doesn't ring

* The time and space stretches out before you unfilled

* You have no deadlines, no reason to hurry

* No one talking to you or at you

* You form no opinions of others. You have no ideas about their situations or how to help them.

Does that sound blissful?

Many elderly people or those confined through illness or disability have this as their daily situation; some without hope of it ever being different.

Although we know this very well, we still find our busy situation intolerable at times. Perhaps what is most difficult is our inability to bring ourselves into balance. This would enable us to face the way life approaches us calmly, no matter whether we are finding this approach over or underwhelming.

But what is the nature of this 'balance' we lack? There is a belief around somewhere that we ought to be able to manage our lives better. There are training courses we can go on entitled 'work/life balance' or something similar.

It might be more useful to sit with the realisation that life manages and uses us – not the other way round.

What we can do is to remain open and non-judgemental with the situations we are given; to be patient and diligent and to do the best we can with what is put our way one thing at a time.

We can be calm in the face of all the requests and demands that are made upon us. None of our situations really 'mean' anything. It is just the way things are and we are just the way we turn out to be (in spite of all our trying), every day until the end of all days.

Don't make the mistake of believing that this is a lazy, couldn't care less, giving up, aimless way of living. To achieve the openness and equanimity required, you must be fully engaged, disciplined and emotionally resourceful.

If you can relax and stop wanting, you will find that this is so and be much more Graceful and content. You have and are everything.

Notes:

86. Stand back, here comes the rescuer

When you discover someone who needs helping, do you feel fully alive, dying to be useful, never needing to be asked twice before rescuing them?

Do you pride yourself on having a kind heart and always being quick to spot someone struggling with something and lending a hand whether they ask for it or not?

Do you feel upset when those you have helped don't seem to be grateful anymore preferring to go it alone without your aid?

Are you conscious of putting your own needs to one side while you show someone else the way out of their crisis?

If the above is true for you, then you may be what could be described as a 'serial rescuer'. The S.R. doesn't actually put their needs to one side at all, despite the way things look at first sight, because their primary need **is** actually to rescue and help others constantly.

Without such acts of 'kindness' to perform, the rescuer doesn't feel complete, useful or loved. Being helpful is the habitual way of getting appreciation used by the rescuer, who is afraid at some level that they are simply not good enough to be loved for just being who they are.

For the unawake rescuer, most of this need-driven helping is unconsciously played out. Usually it takes many experiences of feeling ungratefully treated by people they have inappropriately or over helped to make them wonder what is going on.

So what is going on?

* people in trouble often need just a little help to raise their awareness of resources available. They do not need to be made weaker and more troubled still by becoming dependent on the rescuer.

* rescuers often bury people in tons of help, disempowering them further and attempting to make themselves indispensable.

* when the helped are past their crisis and want to get on with their lives again, the rescuer feels pushed aside and resentful. They can often seduce people back into their uncoping state instead of encouraging and admiring growing independence.

* eventually, it is the rescuer who needs the rescue, not the other way round.

So how has it all come to be this way?

* the natural sweetness of a kind hearted human being has been twisted by a natural but unfulfilled desire to be loved and needed.

* because of their natural aptitude for spotting suffering in others, rescuers have a ready made means for getting this great longing for love met.

* because rescuers are never sufficiently confident that they are just fine and lovable exactly as they are, without doing anything for anyone, they feel obliged to go through their lives trying hard to 'buy' love and gratitude from those that appear to need help.

These attempts to buy love never work in the long term as people that are overhelped usually get fed up with it eventually. When this happens, the rescuer often feels or is heard to say, 'How can you be so ungrateful; I was only trying to help.', or 'After all I've done for you.........'.

If you recognise any of this in yourself, examine your need to be helpful in a gentle way. Kindness is an admirable quality of the heart and the world needs as much kindness as it can get.

But preventing people from gathering strength, making their own way, understanding their own resilience in adversity, standing on their own two feet, forming their own strategies for getting their lives on track, trusting their own judgements about what to do in times of trouble etc., is not kind at all; quite the reverse.

How does it help people to grow if they only get to admire what **you** can do, rather than realise what **they** can do? This is not truly helpful; at least, not to them.

Begin to see your compulsion to rescue as being mostly something about you and your understandable desire to be loved and needed. Whether you know it now or not, you are loveable as you are. There is no need to do anything extra.

When helping anyone else in future, offer the minimum amount that will make a difference and go on your way. That is the most Graceful way of helping. Be like the midwife delivering the baby who afterwards will say, 'Mother did it all herself'.

Notes:

87. Are you drowning in the ocean of your own cynicism?

Is it hard for you to believe in anything? Do you listen to everything that is said to you through the filter of distrust? Are you certain that all information reported in the media is corrupt? Are all those in government incompetent or worse as far as you're concerned?

Do young people today have it far too easy? Are the old living longer and taking up too many hospital beds? Are most drivers not fit to be on the road?

Do you think teachers today don't know how to teach, doctors don't know how to heal and people generally don't know how to behave?

* What is it you are choosing to put your attention on and why?

* Why do you need to be so vigilant and watchful: who are you protecting? Is it you?

* Have you any idea of what it feels like to listen to your opinions on what is wrong with everything on a daily basis? Ask someone you know to tell you.

Your bias (they will fool you or get one over on you if you don't watch out) is running the show, running your life and is the filter through which you see your world. Other people do not have this particular bias and so do not see things in the same way.

In the past your trust might have been repeatedly disappointed and as an antidote to this early experience, you decided to believe very little about anything. That way no-one could fool you or catch you out again. You wouldn't have to cope with the grief of unmanageable disappointment of constantly dashed hopes.

As part of this self-preservation strategy, you developed a particular focus which leads you to concentrate on those issues in life where trusting others is called for. This focus bring reasons not to trust very much to the fore of your consciousness and pushes reasons to trust to the back. Your bias is made up of all those reasons not to trust that your past has painfully shown you. This bias provides the cynical filter through which you see your world.

A way forward (when you feel you can trust it) is to bring yourself into an opinion forming mode based on gathering a wider range of evidence than you currently use.

* Do a reality check. Is it really possible that everyone else is being fooled all of the time?

* Where do you get your evidence from to form an opinion? How much of it comes only from your past experience?

* Take another look: update what you know in the light of the present.

* Listen to yourself and your own cynicism.

* Watch others' reactions to what you say and do? Watch them deciding that they know what you will say before you open your mouth.

* Notice how turned off they are by some of your remarks.

* Be less predictable. Get yourself a new perspective.

It is Graceful and healthy to have an inquiring attitude to life. No-one is asking you to become naïve and to accept absolutely everything at face value. The world is full of shadows and light. Be gently vigilant and develop your trust wisely. Don't drown alone in the ocean of your own cynicism. Smile. If not you, then who?

Notes:

88. What is this day for?

For some of us, our lives run a predictable pattern of getting up,
going to work/getting the children to school, coming home and
going to bed. Within this framework we may enjoy ourselves, or
sometimes not, but our days go inexorably onwards in that familiar
rhythm.

In retrospect, the blocks of time in our lives may be memorable only
as months, seasons or years. Our individual days, unless they prove
to be exceptional, tend to run into a blur.

And yet the 24 hours that form a day and a night are set by nature
and not 'man managed' as weeks and months are. The sun rises
and falls; the moon shows her face and sets. It is not up to us.
Our days are presented to us. But when we look back, we can rarely
remember them or what each one was for.

Perhaps that's because we don't know, or haven't decided (because
it is our choice) what our individual days are for. We all know how
to mark a birthday or an anniversary, whether it be joyous or sad, by
remembering it on the appropriate day. Otherwise, our days are
unmarked and mostly unremarkable to the extent that they slip from
our memories and are lost forever.

* How many of your days can't you remember?

* What percentage of your life is that?

* Are the days of your life adding up to an unmarked, unremarkable
life?

Obviously, lives are full of routine matters that have to be attended
to. The lack of stimulus during repetitive tasks switches us off and

we leave, (energetically speaking). No wonder we can't remember what we have done most of the time as we are hardly there.

Attempt to be more present, even when what you are doing is routine. There are new things to be found, even in performing actions you have done many times before. It is not your work that is boring – it is you! The way you apply yourself gives no meaning to what you do. You render your day meaningless. Set about changing that today:

* Quite apart from what you are doing in the next 24 hours to come, dedicate your day to something specific: patience, kindness, clarity, peace etc. If you can, find a few moments to sit quietly and commit your day to your chosen dedication. Revisit your dedication in the little spaces in your day. Say something like: 'I dedicate this day to peace. I will notice peaceful actions happening all around me and hold peace in my heart and mind today'.

* Decide on a goal for your day: one thing you wish to achieve or do before you go to bed. Give yourself just a slight stretch of a goal. Don't make it impossible. Perhaps you have been putting off writing a letter or making a phone call, taking clothes to the cleaners or cooking a favourite desert or cake.

If every day of your life is dedicated to something worth while and you are able to have a goal: something you want to achieve before you go to bed, your days will become more memorable and you will become less bored and boring.

Being present and making each day for something means that you have to show up in your own life. After all, who will live your days if you don't? If not you, then who?

Notes:

89. Is there something missing?

Do you ever have the feeling that your life would be just perfect if only you had more money, a partner, a more interesting job, a bigger house, could lose a few pounds?

This feeling of lack of one important thing, or many things from a life, has a profound effect on how that life is lived and enjoyed. For some people, it seems impossible to be anything but depressed or sad because of the things they feel they don't have. In addition, the feeling of being without; of having something vital missing, is seen as an understandable cause of suffering in ourselves and others.

We accept that it is reasonable to be sad because there is something or someone missing from our lives. We behave as if we have had to make the ultimate sacrifice because we feel we need things that we haven't got. Do you feel this way? Then consider this:

* It is **not** reasonable to be sad because we feel we lack.

* Whatever we feel we lack, what is truly missing is love: love of our lives and love of ourselves.

* There is nothing missing that truly matters or we wouldn't still be living.

* There is always more stuff to be had: that doesn't mean we should or could have it.

* If we had everything that we feel is lacking from our lives, we would still feel that there is something else missing.

True happiness is not dependent on what we are able to get for ourselves or what we are without. It depends on our view of ourselves – which is different to what we actually have or don't have. Our view of ourselves and our lives as a bounty or a sacrifice is not connected to what we actually have, although we often persuade ourselves that it is.

If our view is that our life is a sacrifice without the things we want or need, we would eventually feel that way whatever our true circumstances might be. If our view is that we are fortunate and that life gives us what we need, we would feel that way even if we had very little.

* What does your view consist of: bounty or sacrifice?

If you don't like the way you view your life: if everything looks like lack to you, then change the way you look at it. See things from another angle. Put your attention on what you have been given, not what you have had to give up or have had taken from you.

If you constantly find yourself longing for more of this or less of that, stop wishing your life away and appreciate it instead. Your life is a clear container for your consciousness and Grace. Don't muddy it with your wanting. Just get on and live it.

Notes:

90. One small thing….

It's dark and very early. I'm shivering and waiting for the first train.
Why am I working when it's Sunday? The train is dirty and some
other passengers are sleeping while last night's drinkers are still
noisily making their way home.

It will be a long day: some of the students are feeling very
emotional, the team is ragged and not really pulling together. Why
am I doing this?

My train pulls into Waterloo station. I had hoped to go directly by
tube, but no, engineering works have closed the line so I go the long
way round instead. I walk across the dark station concourse, my
bags are heavy and my boots pinching my toes.

I see a coffee shop that is miraculously open and I go in and order a
cappuccino. I sit outside in the cold watching the other trickle of
travellers pass by. I put my hands around my cup and sip. When I
look up I feel the smile starting in my stomach.

Gradually, the station lights go on and more people pass by. I think
about my father and my sister and notice I am planning to do
something nice for them. I watch a family and observe how careful
the parents are with the children.

A pigeon sits on my foot. It tickles and against the laws of public
hygiene, I slip it a few crumbs as a reward for its cheekiness.

I remember an outing I'm anticipating with a friend next week. I
notice with astonishment that I am feeling very happy. Now when
and how did that happen? Was it there all the time under my
grumpiness, or was it a new feeling coming in with that first sip of
coffee?

Whatever it was that did happen, it was suddenly very easy to let go of my dissatisfaction and feel flooded with generosity, love and belongingness.

It was so easy. So why don't I do it more often: just let my natural happiness burst through and flood me. Why don't you?

* notice what reconnects you to yourself and others in the world

* sadness is always about disconnection

* disconnection is an illusion. Deliberately reconnect and be happy

Notes:

91. Appreciation of the whole

To suggest that every living being is whole, may be very hard to accept for you. To suggest that you are whole may feel impossible.

* How can I be whole when I sometimes lie?

* How can she be whole when she is so ill?

* How can he be whole when he is dying?

* How can they be whole when they are at war?

The things and ideas that we generally use to decide whether something or someone is whole and perfect are nowhere near fundamental enough to be accurate. In the more Graceful measure of our selves, our illnesses and bad behaviour are too superficial to count.

Wholeness and perfection has so many sad disguises.

We must learn to look through or beneath the disguises to get to the wholeness of the way we were created and its perfection. How do we do this?

* Consider the body. Although it is the container for our lives and very precious to us, it can get old and break down in a variety of ways. Can you imagine a better place for us to live in this life? Even in its sickness and tendency to 'depreciate', no-one has yet come up with a better design or model for the body where we live.

* Think about the mind, the great computer that runs the show while we are busy living. If it were man-made, we would say it was

the work of a genius. (It isn't man-made and it is the work of a genius).

* What about the emotions? They master us until we master them and then inform and enrich our lives if we will let them.

The body, the mind and emotions are valuable possessions that make it possible for us to exist here on this earth. They are necessary, but they do sometimes obscure our real wholeness and perfection in a variety of difficult disguises including illness, violence and unhappiness. So what else is there?

Those of you who have seen the dead body of a loved one will know that you are looking at something less than what they were; it becomes apparent that something has left. The principle that animates the body and gives it life – you may call it the Soul, Life-force or Spirit – is no longer present in the corpse.

It is this principle (I will call it the Soul) that is the whole and perfect giver of Grace and Life to every one of us. No matter what temporary distress, sickness, character flaw or other difficult way of being human afflicts us, we each are brought to life by the same animating principle that is Graceful in its potential to be whole and perfect.

Once you believe you are This, you know your own wholeness and that of everyone and everything else.

How does perfection live? Watch yourself and find out.

Notes:

92. Nothing to give; nothing to offer

Sometimes we feel so empty, so unresourced that we aren't able to think of anything we can extend to anyone else. The energy required to speak of our condition, or move to change it seems entirely lacking. We may feel frozen or in a state of shock.

Perhaps we have encountered trouble or fear in our lives. Something may have happened to us or someone we love.

We are in a low, physically de-energised state and wonder how long it will last before we feel ourselves again.   At these times it is important to make little deals with ourselves to take small actions and to do these in the right order.

If the body is reluctant to kick start itself after suffering upset, shock or disappointment forcing it to act is too cruel. Begin this way:

* recognise that the mind and body have been shocked by what has happened and are endeavouring to come to terms with it.

* be kinder to yourself and do what has to be done in small steps

* eat small meals of tasty nourishing food and drink

* get plenty of sleep and pay attention to dreams

* wear soft, comfortable clothes

* begin to write down what has happened to you in your own words

* take gentle physical exercise in the fresh air

* try to make the effort to move yourself geographically from the scene of your upset

* gradually take on your normal tasks but in small amounts at a time

* notice the body gradually normalising itself

* tell a friend about your trouble

Gradually step up what you are able to achieve towards normality. Don't underestimate how small knocks and disappointments can affect you, especially if there have been a series of these in your life.

Try not to worry about how low you feel. Just take small steps to recovering your vitality and enjoyment of life. It will all return if you are tender and gently firm with yourself.

Notes:

93. Would you go to any lengths to avoid meeting yourself?

We live in a society where certain things are valued and other things aren't. One of the espoused values today is education and learning. We admire those who have studied in a variety of academic institutions and have the letters after their names that prove that.

Those of us that are interested in personal learning buy books on self development and spend many of our weekends at courses run by this or that guru. If a month passes without spending time in a community or retreat we might begin to feel we are losing the fight to become aware of ourselves and the way to live our lives.

Learning and development is indeed important, but the first and most fundamental learning is about ourselves and the uncomfortable truths that are often avoided in our flurry of educational activity.

* Academics can spend hours debating the theory of this or the politics of that, but the poor are still poor and the hungry still starving. Words, words, words and more words will not feed or clothe them.

* Self-development devotees can spend days silently gazing at each other, while their knowledge of what they are most afraid of remains untouched and avoided.

* The church may spend centuries debating theological issues while members aren't able to relate to themselves, each other or their differences.

Workshops and courses can be interesting and stimulating. But beware becoming a serial workshopper because being alone with yourself is painful or difficult for you..

* Notice how the post-workshop euphoria dips and fades quite quickly after you return home.

* Observe how the course or workshop activity enables you to put your problems behind you for a while. Notice what difficulties still remain after your return home.

I suggest that our own experience of life and the ways in which we cannot or will not meet ourselves is the starting point for learning. In the business of our search to educate and give meaning to the world, we avoid the education of our own souls and the meeting with ourselves and our own lives. This cannot be given to us by others; amazing teachers though they may be.

With diligence and discipline you can meet yourself in your own life and experience yourself as the subject matter of your most important learning. Do this:

* Trust yourself but constantly question 'what is going on for me now?'

* When you are fooling yourself or avoiding something difficult, begin to recognise the physical feeling of dissatisfaction this generates in your body.

* Ask yourself, 'What am I most afraid of at this moment? What would I do/how would I act if that fearful thing did indeed happen to me?'.

*Recognise your own strategies for coping and do the thing you are afraid of a little at a time (or all at once if you can).

Begin to see the simple and disciplined observation of your own life experiences and avoidances as the primary learning activity you will undertake. Everything else you do may be enjoyable, challenging, expensive, useful or not. Everything else you do will be secondary.

Start by seeing yourself as the primary educator of your soul. You will gradually become aware of your soul as She allows herself to be know by you and thereby becomes your true and Graceful teacher. Notes:

94. The gift of receiving

Most of us love receiving presents and treats from our friends and families at Christmas and birthdays. A huge industry has grown up around the choosing, wrapping and sending of presents to other people. We are encouraged to be 'generous' and to run up large bills on our credit cards in order to do this.

But what about those gifts we get for free; the gifts beyond price which are our skills, attributes, positive attitudes and characteristics, the potential for which is present at our birth? These gifts, don't show up on a credit card bill, yet may be dearly won as we attempt to manifest these in a society which may or may not appreciate them.

Why do many of us have to struggle to find a place in the world where we can put those unique gifts to good use. Surely there is so much need on earth that all our skills could be utilised by someone, somewhere?

* Do you know you are good at something but despair of ever being able to use it in the world?

* Are you a secret musician, artist, storyteller, wizard with numbers, encyclopaedia of general knowledge or negotiator and still have to do a job that uses none of what you are best at because it feels as if no-one wants it?

* Do you have to struggle to have your foremost talent recognised because you are good at 'it' but bad at marketing yourself?

* Does no-one want your treasure?

Then understand that usually, the pain isn't about not being able to get paid for doing what you are most skilled at, it's about having no-one to do it for: no-one to receive your gifts; no-one to recognise them and therefore you.

A talent becomes a gift when there is a recipient. If there isn't anyone to acknowledge, receive, recognise and appreciate, the gift can be offered, but not given. Perhaps then, the most fortunate attribute that a human being can be blessed with at birth is the gift of being able to receive.

Such receiving is sadly rare. It is extraordinary in its tendency to spot the unique gift being offered in the person of another individual and to accept it and them in their entirety, wasting nothing. Receiving in this way isn't like a pick and mix – taking this bit, leaving that - using this, rejecting that – needing a person's gifts then and not needing them now.

This kind of receiving is not a similar process to borrowing books from a lending library. You borrow the books for you. When you receive a being's gifts, you do it for them.

Consider that when you receive a person's gifts it isn't primarily for you at all, it is to enable them to give themselves and be seen by you for what they truly are. When we are truly seen and received, then we grow, become and blossom, knowing that what we bring is of use in the world. In the mirror of another's regard we see and understand the nature of our gifts and our purpose in the world.

Don't underestimate your responsibility in growing humankind. Start receiving the gifts offered to you by others with all the Grace you can muster. Consider this responsibility as sacred. There is much to do and have and give. Even though we may be welcomed to the world as babies, this welcoming and receiving needs to happen continuously throughout life as we grow and become more and more of ourselves.

Every stage of our personal evolution requires a Witness. We all deserve to be received for who we are and what we bring. What can you do to bring this about?

Notes:

95. Intoxicated by the prospect of the worst

Someone has died a 'romantic' death: illness, over a period of time - gently fading with many visitors to the bedside - bravely facing the worst with great courage - the planning of one's own funeral and the giving away of personal possessions - intoxicating in its specialness and beauty.

By contrast creatures and people and situations carry on until they don't. Existence and everyday life can be humdrum until death intervenes. The getting up and the going to bed are sometimes tedious and often unexciting. Steadiness and sameness are things we avoid. We are often drawn to the prospect of the worst - the drama, the crisis, the finality, the end of days. Why are we determined to ignore the ordinariness of most of our existence?

What is it in us that often finds the 'worst' more stimulating than the ordinary? What is it about 'ordinary' that we try to avoid when we are glued to the news on TV or the newspaper headline about the latest sad story? Do we prefer to be horrified rather than unstimulated? It seems so.

Why is it that we label our lives 'boring' when we are simply following a pattern of night after day for a period of time?

Non-stimulation has come to mean a wasted life in the popular way of looking at things. No-one wins a prize for living the most ordinary life possible. Lots of prizes are won by being the most this or the least that. Even infamy in praise of mass cruelty brings notoriety. I know of no-one famous for living an ordinary life.

What would excellence look like in an ordinary life. What would an exemplary life lived ordinarily consist of?

Perhaps acceptance of one's ordinariness in the great scheme of things would be a start? Then you or I might have to maintain some humour to balance the popular view of the world that our lives were unexceptional and that we were seen as rather dull. Eventually it might be a good idea to educate others about the qualities of the ordinary life that they could emulate and perhaps adopt.

At the danger of losing sight of my own ordinariness I might risk starting up a movement in praise of the ordinary and insignificant. Potential devotees could be screened for their willingness to become dull too. At the end of their training, they could assume the title of The Dull Mr Brown or the Ordinary Miss Smith. There is no end to the money that could be made and the communities that might be born.

But that would probably be the end of the simple ordinariness of my life. Just another ploy Jan. You've been sussed!

Notes:

96. Getting your agreements clear

Do you stand by the agreements you have made or do you sometimes forget to check the detail of what you have said you will do for or with others?

* do you assume you know what it is that the other person is expecting of you without checking?

* do you think you know what they believe things will be like when you have completed what you said you would do?

* do others often say something like, 'I thought you meant that you would do **that** and you've done **this**'?

We often believe we know what is in another's mind; what they mean by what they say. This belief is usually based on what we would have thought and meant under the same circumstances. Of course, this is an assumption and often an inaccurate one at that.

The range of human responses to a particular situation is wide and varied.   It is probably safer to assume nothing than to think we are completely aware of another's expectations without checking.

The agreements we might make on a daily basis can be simple ones or quite complex. They can be as different as these:

* Can you pick my dry cleaning up for me please?
* Could you help me shop for my wedding and bridesmaids' dresses?
* Will you put together a proposal for restructuring the department?

The above three requests differ in complexity and scale, but all have some components that are the same. Checking out the other person's expectations will help you to know whether and how you will agree to do it or not. Find out about:

* timescale: by when do they want it to be done? Perhaps their timescale is tight and they want you to do it now. The dry cleaning might be wanted for tonight and tomorrow might be too late. Before agreeing to fetch it you need to know that.

* scope: Is the proposed wedding shopping something that might need several trips to town over a number of weekends or has the bride already selected something and simply wants you to approve her choice? If so the time commitment you are agreeing to will be quite different.

* purpose: In order to achieve what? Would your work on the restructuring proposal form the basis for a downsizing or cost cutting exercise or would it change working practices or expose a need for new equipment? Be clear what your work is intended to achieve.

* resources: What do you need to complete the agreement you are about to make? Will you need to take the car to get the dry cleaning, wear flat comfortable shoes for going from shop to shop with the bride, or reserve space and time to complete the work project?

* how will you know when your agreement is complete? Will this be when the bride has found a number of dresses to try on for her mother or when she buys her gown and takes it home? When you hand your proposal over to your boss will that mean that the job is complete or will he want to agree it and come back to you with suggested amendments. Perhaps he may want you to present your proposal to other senior people?

So you can see from the above that it isn't surprising that we sometimes disappoint others and that they confuse us.

* They thought they had made themselves clear.

* We thought we knew what they meant.

* They were sure they could count on us to do **that**

* We know we said that we would do **this**

Doing the checking can feel a bit cumbersome sometimes, but it is worth getting clear. Cut down on the number of times you find yourself doing something you wish you had said no to. Not keeping your agreements can ruin your reputation with others. Make sure you know what you are agreeing to. Get crystal clear.

Notes:

97. So you think you are a leader?

We tend to value the people who, single-handedly, can get things done; change the world, win the race, become millionaires, step forward and make it all happen.

Certainly these individuals have a powerful energetic thrust towards being top of the pile, the chosen one: the guy or girl in the lead who collects followers wherever they go. They have push and shove power and describe themselves as strong personalities. They are often able to make things happen by getting people to do what they want.

They wear their power on the outside and it is often driven by their ego's desire to use and manipulate others (albeit in subtle ways), if they believe the end justifies the means.

* Are you the charismatic type that people allow to tell them what to do?

* Are you acutely aware of your position, the hierarchy and keeping control of what you have built and therefore believe to be yours?

* Do you watch for usurpers, those who are trying to take control from you?

* Do you have a parental concern for your 'followers', ensuring they are rewarded when they behave or deliver?

For such people working collaboratively, cooperating with others rather than leading them from the front and genuinely sharing the leadership position is either extremely uncomfortable or impossible.

The reason given for not allowing others to lead the way by sharing power is that 'they aren't up to it'.

How do people become 'up to it' if they aren't given a chance? What a true leader is able to do is to practice 'power with' rather than 'power over'. People become 'up to it' very quickly when served by such a leader because they can step forward into their own power and skill without fear of encountering disappointment, (I trusted you and you let me down), punishment or criticism.

A true leader shares power with others: not taking it back or personally when things go wrong, but collaborating with others and coordinating the upsurge of their abilities and skill.

They do not believe that the organisation/group/family that they are serving is theirs: they know it exists because others share the journey and is an entity in its own right. Who founded it is of little importance: how the power is shared within it today is paramount.

Such leaders are not usually charismatic in worldly ways; their egos don't require constant stroking by being seen to lead. Their primary concern is for the sharing of power with, and the Graceful growth of all.

This is true Grace in leadership, which requires maximum personal maturity and minimum adoration from other people. Do you know anyone like that? Could you do it?   If not you, then who?

Notes:

98. Unhappiness can be hard to part with

We imagine that to be happy in our lives is what we wish for. Sometimes, though, it doesn't turn out quite that way.

 Some of us have had a long term sadness in our lives which has become so familiar that we begin to shape our lives around it and to accommodate it in all sorts of ways, rather than to choose to move towards happiness and a different way of being.

Being unhappy long term can give your life a certain character and might mean that there are things you habitually do or don't do:

* Do you always turn down invitations for dinners, parties or celebrations to the extent that people no longer ask you?

* Do you rarely wear bright colours or use vibrant shades to decorate your home?

* Have you stopped buying or arranging treats for yourself?

* Have you begun to see others' happiness in a certain light; perhaps cynically or disbelieving, thinking 'They'll soon see, It won't last?'

* Do you believe that you aren't good company and avoid people?

* Do you sometimes acknowledge how much you like to be left alone and are satisfied with your own company?

The slow and still character to an unhappy life can become familiar and welcome to people who have been unhappy for a long time to the extent that they no longer hope nor wish for change.

It's a bit like getting stuck in something grey and rather viscous: easier to stay there than shake free and climb out of it.

This means that even though it would now be possible to allow the sadness to fall away and to get on with a different sort of life, some people resist the change to stay with the known and thereby waste an opportunity to move towards something lighter.

If this is you, try taking small steps towards the light. The following self-directions might be a place to start:

* My sadness has served its purpose now.

* Now I am better and can lead a lighter life whenever I wish.

* I can let my life be Graced by others, one by one.

* I can take part in others' lives a little at a time.

Find one small thing that you can do differently every day: smile at one person, say hello, talk to people who serve you in shops, ask someone something about themselves. Practice being happy if it no longer comes naturally to you. It soon will.

Don't consider yourself in an unhappy frame any more. Think of yourself as leaving that state behind. Take the risk to gradually become happier in little ways. Kick your addiction to unhappiness out of your life. Step out of the 'goo' and begin to live in the light.

Notes:

99. Hospitality of the Heart

Are you one of those who love having people round to dinner or to stay in your home? You like to be hospitable and take pains to make sure guests have everything they need.

For the next few moments, I want you to consider a different, or deeper type of caring, that I call hospitality of the heart. This is not so much about the care of people who are guests in your home, (although it can be extended to those people too), as the care of those who are temporarily or permanently guests in your life.

Whereas you might try to find out what guests to your home like to eat and how they usually live in order to make them most comfortable, hospitality of the heart offers an acceptance of who each guest truly is and a welcoming for them as unique and perfect.

We cannot be truly hospitable if we look at people who meet us as creatures with flaws that need mending or putting right. Begin to develop a hospitable heart when your are with others in this way:

* Open up the ears to listen without listening for anything in particular. Just hear

* Open up the eyes to see what is there without wishing to improve or change what you see in the other. Just look.

* Open the lips to say 'I see', 'I hear', 'I accept you as you are'. Speak nothing but acknowledgement.

* Open up the heart in gratitude for he or she that comes as a guest-in-trust to the home of your life.

True hospitality is the understanding that guests come into your life to enrich it. It is they that have come to give, not you. Your task is to open fully to the experience of the encounter and accept exactly what is brought to you, without judgement of its worth.

Just have the Grace to accept what is given. Don't judge the worth of the gift of each human being that comes as a guest, whether they stay for seconds or a lifetime. That is not your business. Your business is to be awake to them and receive.

Notes:

100. We 'needs must love'......

The poet Tennyson wrote: 'We needs must love the highest when we see it...'. What does 'the highest' mean to you?

* Your God?

* Your family?

* Your career?

* Your tv set?

* A favourite piece of music or work of art?

As we go through our lives, 'the highest' may change. From a boyfriend or girlfriend in adolescence, our focus may shift to a partner or a child. Others might value their work more highly than anything else in their lives. Some people never seem able to move away from the accumulation of wealth as the highest and central tenet of their existence.

It is tempting to make judgements about what people love most. At first consideration, it seems more worthy to put your family first and to love it than to value a career, study or money. Perhaps it might be interesting to look at **what** we see in our 'highest' that makes us love it.

Sometimes we see things that we can have: security, ego-satisfaction, fulfilment of duty, a cure for loneliness, fears for the future. A religion, a family or money could all fulfil that need in us.

But sometimes we can clearly see the movement of Spirit and Grace in that which we consider 'the highest'. This beautiful reflection could appear to us in our partner, our stocks and shares, a work of art or the work we do every day.

Look again at that which you consider to be 'the highest':

* to what extent does it speak to and move your soul?

* if your 'highest' is a person, look past their surface beauty which you will soon become used to: how much of what you truly love is Spirit moving in them?

* if your choice is money or some other worldly thing, is it being put to a Graceful use and is this what you love about it ?

Become less interested in whether it is right or wrong to love something and concentrate on what is inherent in your love for you to put it 'highest'.

When your 'highest' is shown to you, love it and give yourself to it. Commit to it and consider it as your refuge.   If it turns out that you have been mistaken in what you held to be highest, that is alright too. You will recover and find a more worthy love.

Notes:

101. Disbelieve what you believe

Look out at your favourite view. Then close your eyes and blot it
out. How do you know that it is still there when you aren't looking
at it? Could it be that it is your act of looking that creates what you
are looking at? How can you be sure? Think about it.

We are far too sure that we know how things are most of the time.
Indeed knowing for sure is a 'quality' that is highly valued today.
People who say that they don't know are often thought to be ill
informed. However, these people are probably nearer to the Truth
than most.

It makes sense to know some sorts of facts: what time is the train,
is this substance safe etc? But that life and its meaning remain
pretty much of a mystery for our discovery and rediscovery rather
than knowing it off by heart isn't generally appreciated. We aren't
supposed to know everything about everything. We are designed to
remain curious and constantly explore.

The trouble is that when we reach a point of knowing something
that we feel comfortable with, we feel so relieved to be rid of the
discomfort of not knowing, that we hold fast to the rightness of our
idea. This holding fast sets the idea firmly within us. Then we build
up other ideas around it. Soon we have the original idea in the
middle of a supporting structure of belief that helps to keep it proven
and unquestionable. Over time we cease to reconsider our belief in
our original idea and it becomes part of who we are.   It would take
something huge to make a dent in that wouldn't it?

Do you have beliefs like that, built of ideas and supported by yet more ideas until you convince yourself that this is Truth rather than just ideas or opinions? Think about it:

* What do you know that you are so sure of that you no longer return to it and question?

* How long have you believed some of your 'favourite' beliefs and views? When did you last revisit them?

* What ideas do you have that you hold as sacrosanct? What might happen if you took another good, long look?

* Do you value yourself for what you know? If you didn't know those things or they were proved to be incorrect or unimportant, would you feel less valuable as a person?

Where is the inquiring one in you? When you were a child that one helped you investigate your world with fascination and awe. You weren't concerned with whether you knew or didn't know then. Each day was a piece of research into wonder. What happened to that?

Perhaps when you went to school you realised that some of your ideas about things were thought of as right and some seemed to be labelled 'wrong'. Being right soon became more important to you than being a permanent inquirer into life. So you learnt to get it right as often as you could and you're still doing that now.

But nothing we believe is as it seems. The rightness and sureness that is worshipped now is a mistake and suggests that everything is static; frozen in time. The fact is that we live in a magical and changeable universe where even the material from which everything, including ourselves, is made, is in constant motion and flux.

If your ideas about life that is ever moving stay fixed, you are just not keeping up are you? Practice some disbelief: throw your ideas up in the air occasionally and see what comes down. Give the sceptic in you a treat. Do it quickly before your intelligence sets like concrete and the inside of your head becomes a museum!

Notes:

102. Why do you pretend to love what you hate?

Sometimes we call doing what we hate 'duty'. We do things day after day that bring us no joy and we console ourselves that we are good people when we do this. We are sure that when we fulfil our obligations, as we see them, even if that drags us down and makes us life-weary, that is what we should be doing. We become martyrs and that is all the reward we can hope for.

But to who or to what is our highest obligation due?

* our parents, partners or our children?

* our values and beliefs?

* our jobs or careers?

These calls upon us are important and to suggest otherwise would be unrealistic, but our highest obligation is to something less tangible and more permanent.   Some might call this Spirit or Soul, or simply the force of Life that breathed us into this existence.

Whatever you call **It**, you owe it everything. Most of all you owe it your joy; that symptom of a Graced state of living. Joy is not happiness or jollity or having a good time. Joy is not necessarily exhibited by laughing, giggling or smiling. Joy is not necessarily attached to any particular thing or elicited by an absence of sorrow. Joy is as light as a bubble: a refusal to be anything other than itself and to be weighed down by no-thing. It is your first 'duty' to your true birther: Life.

Once your first 'duty' is fulfilled, everything else will either fall into place behind it or fall away.   You will cease to do anything in the way you once felt you had to. You will stop pretending to love doing the things you hate. You will stop violating yourself with your notions of what you 'should' do. You will live a Graceful life.

A life bound to joy serves everything it touches in a completely unselfish and generous way. Therefore there is never a need for such a life to concern itself with duty.

What viable alternative is there now you know? You can't keep on violating your Soul and pretending not to notice.

You can't continue to pretend that you love what you hate and that everything is fine with you when it isn't. There is a debt to be paid to Life in terms of your health, happiness and well-being.

* Nice people pay their debts.

* It is in this Life that you can drop the duty. Future lives are all so uncertain.

Notes:

103. Make sure your head is on the right way round!

I watched a large group of people recently, being given a chance to have a hand in shaping their own destiny.

What did they do: (not all of them but enough to have a real affect on the proceedings), they moaned about the past.

The complaining voices were louder and more insistent than those of us who wanted to start something new, so the whole proceedings in retrospect felt full of remorse about what had happened in the past.

Instead of looking towards the front of things, too many of us habitually turn round and face the other way. Until we grow eyes in the backs of our heads, the only way we can look forwards in those circumstances is to go backwards without a clear view of where we are going to.

Obviously, if people harbour hurts it is sometimes difficult to move past these: difficult but not impossible.

It really does depend on what you want most; to face backwards or move forwards. The energy raised from forward movement can often be used to heal the past simultaneously. We do not always need to be conducting post mortems. New avenues and experiences provide a seed bed for doing things differently from before and help to reinterpret bad experiences through new frameworks and fresh perspectives.

There is only so much backward facing that can be done positively. Most of us benefit from turning round to face our future and a new perspective in this life, rather than waiting for natural selection to produce beings with eyes in the backs of their heads.

Notes:

104. If only ……

If only your life wasn't so difficult. If only there weren't quite so many things stacked up against you being happy. If only everything was less problematic!

If only there weren't so many reasons 'why not'.

Did you get up this morning feeling glad to be alive, or did you drag yourself from your bed feeling heavy and weighed down? If I asked you what was preventing you from being happy would you tell me something like this:

* …if only I could find somewhere else to live…

* …but I can't do that because I don't have enough money…

* …can't get a better job to earn more because I live too far from the city….

* …won't move into the city until I get a better job…

and on and on.   In this sort of scenario we build up a huge sticky net of reasons why we can't do what we want to do. Our response to any offer or helpful suggestion tends to be, 'I could, yes, but…'. All we can produce is reasons 'why not'.

We give the fact that we are suffering from so many different difficulties and problems in our lives as the reason we can't begin to shift them. We are weighed down under the burden of layers of difficulty and can't see where to make a start to improve things. So we do nothing except moan about it.

Our belief that we have many problems is a mistake. We have only one. The one we have is an important one that affects everything we will ever do in our lives to change things for the better. The one problem we have is that we will not give up our fear in order to put an end to our suffering.

What is the nature of this fear we won't give up:

* we are fearful because we don't know what will happen if we stop being afraid

* we are afraid because we may hurt others or gain their disapproval if we stop being scared and make the changes we say we want

* we are frightened of how expanded and new our lives might become if we lose our fear and move forward

So we hold on to all our problems tightly because in their way they are a defence against fearless living. We continue to suffer because we are afraid to surrender to our fear and just step forward into the freedom of living truly.

How long will you continue to make your excuses? How many times will you say 'yes but', to the world? When will you surrender and say, 'Yes Please'?

Notes:

105. The strength of gentleness

When you consider the word 'strength' what images come to mind.
Perhaps you think of bulging muscles, powerful physiques, high
energy, loud voices? Let's take a few moments to explore what
strength in ourselves and our own lives might be like and what other
images we can bring to mind to do that.

* What is common in some of the popular images of strength listed
above?

All the images above bring to mind a force or push energy. If there
is nothing for such energy to push against, it has no strength of its
own. The prize fighter needs a fight: no fight – no prize! The
powerful executive needs a result: no result – no power.

If you depend upon your ability to force, whether this force is
energetically physical, mental or emotional, it only works if there is
something to apply it to: it is conditional and bullish.

It isn't only individuals that can rely on making their way in the world
using the energy of force. Whole corporations, certain political
groups and even towns and cities are bullish too. Stand in a noisy
city centre with traffic racing round you, people pushing by you,
flashing lights and advertisements dazzling you, noise and loud
music blaring forth from every shop doorway and feel the wearying
effect of being pushed around by a bullish society.

* So if force isn't strength, what is?

Strength proceeds from a sense of having no fear that you will able
to survive and thrive without having to force anyone to do or think
anything. There is much more strength in meeting the world
without force, but with gentleness. The type of gentleness I am
referring to is the kind that comes from an absence of the desire to
drag, push and shove. This is not the same as being a pushover!

* How can you be gentle and not be seen as weak?

Given that such gentleness comes from an absence of fear, how can it be weak? Be clear that force always proceeds from some sort of fear. That might be:

* fear that you won't do what you need to do unless I make you

* fear that you need me to be strong for you

* fear that really I am terrified and I can't let you see that

* fear that you won't buy what I'm selling unless I coerce you into a result

Once you have a quiet self assurance that you are a unique and valuable being, there need be no fear of what others think. You have no need to act out to win over anyone, force others into a 'good' impression of you or be anything other than who and what you are.

There is a huge strength in Graceful self-assurance. This gentleness proceeds from a still strong centre that no amount of force can push over.

If you are being coerced by something or someone else, try to spot their particular fear beneath the energy of rush, noise, push and bluster.   Be grateful that you don't have that particular frailty and with compassion for yourself and the other, move yourself to higher ground.

Notes:

106. What do you bring to the party?

What is it you do supremely and uniquely well? Often this question
sends people off scratching their heads and wondering. Usually they
come back to say, 'Well nothing much really. I do this or that, but
lots of other people do what I do. There is nothing unusual about
what I do at all.'.

The mistake that people make when they are thinking this way goes
like this:

* We think of what we do rather than how we do it

* We are so used to doing what we do that we no longer consider it
at all – we just do it

* Familiarity with ourselves and our lives 'breeds self-contempt' and
everyone else's life and work looks far more interesting.

Sometimes when I am in a queue at the supermarket I watch the
people operating the tills. What I notice is that although they are
doing more or less the same thing, the way they do it is very
different.

Some till operators interact with each customer, they make eye
contact, they smile, they say good morning and goodbye. Others do
this only if the customer speaks to them first and yet others are in a
world of their own. They process the customer's goods, but
otherwise give no sign that they know there is a human being
standing in front of them.

Perhaps the work you do is a little repetitive or there are many
others doing the same thing as you. It is tempting to think that you
do just the same as they do; that you bring no individuality or
personality to the tasks you do.

Take another look. There will be valuable uniqueness that you bring
to your role. It is a good thing for you to become aware of it so that
you can practice a little self-appreciation once in a while. Doing this

also eases any boredom you might feel about doing the same jobs over and over again.

Begin to see what you do for work, however humble, as a reflection of you and your special human qualities. You don't have to do highly paid work to feel good about your career. It is up to you to invest yourself in your work life and bring all of yourself to whatever you are doing at any moment. The amount of money paid to you doesn't equate to the true value of what you do.

The investment you make in your work is possibly the largest investment in terms of your time that you will ever make. It doesn't make sense to spend all that time wishing you were doing something else.

If what you do really doesn't please you, stop moaning and do something else. Whatever you decide to do for work do it fully and don't spend the time watching the clock. Bring all of yourself to the party. Become really skilled at doing what you do whatever it is.

Notes:

107. Bless all who mother

Many of us are mothers. And some of those are the ones who gave birth and some aren't. Some of us are women and some aren't. Some of us who gave birth find mothering too difficult to contemplate and others who mother naturally and constantly may be men, or women who will never have a child.

The instinct to mother: to nurture, grow and protect is present in varying degrees in humans and animals. The instinct to be mothered is there from time to time in most of us. Some of us need it, some of us give it and others can feel both.

When we separate the desire to nurture from the act of physically giving birth to a baby, we begin to recognise it in a variety of forms:

* the preparation of food, lovingly cooked and offered

* the care of the younger or less experienced ones

* providing the elderly with comfort and shelter

* pastoral care for students, prisoners or congregations

* a listener for the distressed ones

* nursing for the sick

The essence of what we call mothering is the desire to extend oneself in order to provide what is needed for another to grow and thrive; to put another's needs before our own; not to eat before others are fed.

This Graceful and nurturing quality isn't always valued in a society where self and self's needs are often put first. We are losing sight of something so important that humankind will be much poorer for its loss. Paying for someone else to do our nurturing for us, so that we can do something more interesting, robs us of the opportunity to be fully human.

By contrast if we become overburdened in our care for others our 'mothering' becomes mechanical and duty ridden. It is better to get help than to become worn out. Real nurturing has no resentment in it: a resentful 'mother' bakes a bitter meal.

Value the nurturing you receive and bless the one that gives it, whether they are a he or a she, your birth mother or a stranger.

Notes:

108. Weary of what?

What is it we are tired of when we feel weary, day after day.

* Not getting enough sleep?

* Not getting enough opportunities?

* Not being able to think of a better way?

The numbing weariness that settles upon us when we feel we have no power to alter things for the better for ourselves, is like a glue. However much we try to shake it off, it seems to stick to us and prevent action; either emotional of physical.

What is the power that we think we lack? As we begin to notice what we see as repeated disappointment, our faith in ourselves and a beneficent world fades away. Grace, working through our intuitive sense is telling us what to do and what not to do about our situation, but we are too sleepy to maintain the awareness that intuition needs to make itself heard or felt.

The sense of powerlessness to make anything better for ourselves is so painful for us that we begin to go to sleep. Weariness, although inconvenient, is less troublesome to us than living daily with an idea of our own lack of power.

What can be done?

* Accept offers of help even if you aren't sure you can be bothered

* Stay awake and aware for one hour and during that time listen for guidance from Grace working through intuition

* During your wide awake hour, ask 'What must I do now?'. Repeat the question until you get an answer. It will come if you are patient, but be prepared for the answer to be wordless.

* Take a short spell of exercise every day.

World weariness can be a symptom of your own disappointment in yourself and what you see as your lack of power. Begin to consider your power as personal. Grace, working through your intuitive sense is always waiting to attract your attention in empowering ways.

Don't say that you don't know what to do. Mostly you do know, but you are unwilling to face the changes that are part of that next step.

The most difficult thing about next steps is the thinking and worrying about them.

The doing is a doddle compared to that.

Notes:

109. Laughter

Life is a very serious business isn't it? No of course it isn't.
Everything we do is extremely important isn't it? No, I'm afraid not.
We have to be very careful to do the right thing in the right way at
the right time don't we? Not really. No.

We endow ourselves and our doings with all kinds of gravitas and
importance. It's hard for us to be simply one of many; no more
interesting, worthwhile or important than any other being, no matter
what our actions or our achievements.

The fear of our own insignificance and mundaneness in the greater
scheme of things is too painful for most of us to bear.

So we strive and struggle to be bigger than, better than and more
achievement ridden than each other rather than face the fact that
you and I are as we are: not one jot more important than each
other and not one scrap more valuable or necessary than when we
arrived in this life and took our first breath.

Now isn't that just one of the funniest things you have ever heard?

We puff ourselves up in the most grandiose ways. Who are we
trying to impress and why?

Let the air out of your body – laugh kindly at yourselves. Laugh
from the very depths of your belly.

I'm afraid you have to accept sooner or later that you are much less
important than you hoped to be but that you are so much more
precious and worthwhile than you can imagine.

Notes:

110. The way we think life should be

When we are young we are full of certainty about the way life should
be. We have our ideals, our hopes, our dreams and our very long
wish lists. All this gives youth and young adulthood an energy and
direction, which can appear very attractive when we look backwards
from our middle years.

As we grow older we realise that some of the things we hoped for
will not happen, but instead of letting those dreams go lightly, we
can become desperate for that last chance to have things the way
we want.

We can become very Saturnian in our own view of our lives: feeling
trapped with the ideas of what we never achieved. Do you have
pain around some of the things you hoped for in your life, which will
not now happen? Do you feel a failure because you weren't able to
make your own, or a loved one's dreams come true? Consider this
way of thinking about the loss of your dreams:

* Some of our ideas about life are most valuable in the letting go of
the dream, not the achievement of it.

* Because we believe that dreams are for coming true instead of
just dreaming, we may miss the point of them altogether.

The things we most strongly believe and the things we most
desperately want tell us so much about our deepest motivations and
desires. Waking dreams, like sleeping ones are often not literal:
sometimes we have them in order to learn things about ourselves
and our world.

We could fulfil a thousand dreams, but the greatest mystery and
prize of all is the knowing of ourselves. Our dreams and ambitions
tell us much about ourselves: our secret desires, our shames, our
love of beauty, our strivings to be better thought of than we are.

* Instead of becoming depressed and cynical about unfulfilled dreams, figure out what that particular idea of how your life could have been was trying to tell you about how to live.

* Accept that those of your hopes that didn't come to fruition weren't necessarily meant to, and look instead at what you're doing with what you got instead

Are you regretting still, after all this time, what didn't happen for you way back then. Acknowledge your ignorance of the meaning of what life did give you, instead of bewailing what it didn't. Dissolve your fixed opinions of what your life should or could have been like. It is not yet too late to learn from what you have been given, but if you are constantly chasing after something else instead, it soon will be.

Notes:

111. Tell your own story

When you look back over your life, does it seem a jumble of happenings, good and bad? Do you have difficulty in fitting things together chronologically? Why not create your own story and set it down in pictures, words, art or music: make a personal ceremonial of your life.

* Collect together all the photographs, music and mementoes you can find.

* Find all the letters, documents, diaries and notes

* Bring out all the small items that have meaning.

Clear a space on the floor and begin arranging them in a time line, from your earlier years to the present. Get things in the right order until it begins to make sense.

* What do you notice most about your time line: the number of relationships, the progression from job to job, births, deaths, marriages?

* What are the themes you notice: are the high spots your travels or your relationships: are the low spots illnesses, bereavements or separations?

* Where or on what have you spent most of your time: friends, work, family, recreation?

* What seems most absent: your spiritual life, stable relationships, homes?

Stand at the beginning of your time line and see your life to the present time stretched out in front of you. Slowly move from life stage to life stage, reliving past experiences from the vantage point of today.

* What do you notice that you never realised before?

* What are the repeating patterns, positive and negative, as you now see them?

When you find yourself back in the present, turn and look back at the journey you have taken.

* What do you want more of in your future that has been scarce in your past?

* What do you want less of from now on, that you had much of before?

If you wish, note down your thoughts and feelings. Remember how your life looked to you, stretched out like a ribbon from your beginning until now. Understand the sense you saw in the way your life was arranged, like a tidal river flowing back to the source from this point.

Be clear that your life has been a masterwork of sense, arranged in such a way that you can learn from your own example whenever you want to. Have the Grace to be grateful for the education you have been given. See your life as a whole, not as a series of random events strung out from there to here. See your investment in it as worthy. Then decide what you want to be next.

Notes:

112. Stepping Forward

It is amazing how our fear can stop us living fully. If we don't put up our hands and say, 'I'll do it!', then we think we can stay safe. We can remain untried and untested and therefore not proved wrong or deficient in some way.

* If I don't tell you what I think, then you can't say that I am wrong

* If I don't show up and show you what I can do, then I won't feel as if I've done badly or not well enough

* If I do nothing, then I can't be accused of making a mistake

What a paralysed life the cage of our fear can create for us. The energy of fear of failing trapped inside us brings about stasis and a curious stalledness to the process of our living.

We are neither right nor wrong. We are neither good nor bad. We are neither truly living nor actually dead. So what are we then?

* We are like wine, fine by reputation, but never tasted

* We are all potential and no actual

* We are all promise and no delivery

* We are all something that does nothing

The release of energy when we step forward into the unknown of how truly Graceful we can be is amazing. Whether our 'performance' is judged to be good or bad by others isn't significant. The vital thing is to act: and in that action to know our own place and purpose in the world and our tribe as One Who Takes Part and Gives.

May the Spirit burn brightly in all who step forward today.

Notes:

113. Blind Spots and Black Holes

Looking back at ourselves without bias is never easy. Over time, and if we are lucky, the reflections back from others mean that we can become better acquainted with ourselves and our impact in and upon the world.

But there are always parts of ourselves that remain hidden from us, whilst exposing themselves and us quite clearly to others. Without help we remain in ignorance of these 'blind spots'.

If we are to grow and become wiser and more whole, the reflecting back of ourselves (sometimes known as feedback) should be actively sought, both from people who appear to agree with us and our views, and those who don't.

Conversely, we should also have the generosity, and take the risk, to offer to reflect back to others the effects they have on us, both positive and less so.

Feedback that is continually complementary is out of balance and therefore of limited value. Those who will give only positives to those they care about may believe they are being kind, but they are mistaken.

Through our connection in humanness, we are all responsible for helping to alert the other to blind spots. We are culpable when we won't find the courage and the tenderness to attempt this task and to do it with straightness.

If we won't add to the information others have about themselves both positive and negative, even though it may give us some discomfort, what is that saying about us? Does it mean we are only ever thinking positive things about others?   No, probably not.

Where is the logic that makes it not ok to think negative thoughts about others, but ok to keep those thoughts to ourselves when they arise?

* The desire to control the information contained in our thoughts and not to share it with the other lacks generosity and courage. It keeps us safe behind the smile.

* Although our reticence to ask the other to consider areas in which they could grow can masquerade as kindness, niceness and a desire to encourage, it mostly encourages only the status quo and more of what already is. It moves nothing, it changes and grows nothing.

Step up and out of the sticky black hole of terminal positivity and give a balanced reflection back to those you profess to care about. Who else will if you don't?

Notes:

114. Shame and other bogeymen

Generally we have little memory of our earliest days so find it hard to recall the feelings we arrived into the world with or developed very soon after. But as we grow older, we begin to realise that there are some powerful feelings that come to us frequently, perhaps from the past, often without appearing to have a correspondingly significant trigger or source in the present.

For example we might sometimes find ourselves feeling a deep and overwhelming shame that seems to be in response to a small error. We wonder why we are feeling so much in response to so little. It makes no sense.

We might find ourselves suffering deep remorse at having committed the slightest of offences. Although we begin to see that this isn't necessary, we don't know why we react in that 'out of proportion' way.

There are a number of theories and ideas of where such unbidden emotional reactions come from and how they are able to afflict us now. These can vary from past life ideas to the taking on of our parents' pain in utero. Also of course, there will be all the earliest experiences of childhood that can seem so traumatic to our infant understanding.

Perhaps the most important thing is to begin to see how we can suffer less shame (or whatever the emotion is for you) when it isn't appropriate to do so.

* The first step is to become aware of shame arising when there is little going on that should prompt that feeling.

* As the shame grows, but before you begin to become distressed by it, remind yourself that, 'this is not mine; I do not have to feel like this'.

* Once you are able to be calm and witness the shame rising rather than being it, tell yourself, 'this is not about now; I do not have to

react in this way'.

* Return to the situation in hand. Decide how you want to deal with it and move on.

You may have to spend quite a bit of time practicing the first step as it requires a swift response and the ability to deal with what is going on in the outer world and what is going on in your inner world simultaneously.

The ability to witness ourselves in the midst of our rising distress is an everyday example of Grace. We cease to be pulled about by our feelings. We become the sensitive, intelligent creatures we were always meant to be.

Living with frequent bouts of disembodied and deep shame denies the beauty and perfection of your existence.

Notes:

115. Get off it and get on

Have you ever felt so angry that you become incandescent in your rage: it feels as if you must surely explode if you can't tell someone what you think of them, stop something from happening or change an unfair or imperfect situation.

Sometimes the anger gets so huge it frightens us. We become afraid of what will come out of us if we do let go.   So we pack it down, sit on it, tell ourselves it will go away.

Even if we are willing and able to talk about what has offended us, others may not be willing to hear, the moment might have passed or we might feel that we lack the power to make a difference in the way we want.

Over time this inability and uncertainty about speaking out can cause us to become weak, disempowered and whiney. We turn our straight and powerful anger into moaning and complaining. Our fiery avenging energy has become a 'poor me' wail.

Having reduced the power of our feelings, we then feel safer to speak about them. We moan and whine and whinge to our nearest, dearest and anyone else who will listen. Most of what we have to say to them begins, 'I can't....', 'Why them and not me.......', 'It's not fair,' etc., etc.

The me-me and I-I focus of the whinger completes the process of their own disempowerment as others have little patience or sympathy for a cause voiced in this manner. People will not listen to someone moaning for long and if they do stick around out of duty, they soon stop hearing.

So when something seems wrong to you and you become angry, how can you use the energy raised in this way in a constructive manner? How do you get people to listen? How do you avoid turning into a moaning whinger?

* Write it, say it, dance it, paint it – but get it out there before it turns into whiney sludge inside you.

* When you want to change something, propose a solution that will do this and benefit everyone – don't put all your energy into moaning about the problem.

* Ride your fierce energy in a creative way: suggest ways to do things that are new and innovative – be willing to start things yourself.

* Don't wait to be invited to do or say things differently – just do it and let people know what you are doing and why

* Drop the done-to or overlooked victim – it's so unattractive to be anywhere near. Burn with the courageous anger of the hero and invite others to help you find better ways to be and do.

* Don't blame the powers that be when you won't take up your own power

* Don't give away your strength and play weak because you are not at the top of your particular hierarchical structure.

* Support others in their attempts and causes, be less competitive. Everyone must have their birthing time: your turn will come.

The force of the energy that comes with anger may be similar to the invisible but clearly discernable rush of Spring energy that brings everything in nature back into being. Go with your own flow. Use your anger creatively. Don't let it rot down into stinky whinging. Get off it and get on – there is so much you can have, and do and change and be. (Unless you'd rather just moan about it of course).

Notes:

116. Attend to your battles and forget the skirmishes

People in relationships often fall out over the most insignificant things. Battle lines can be drawn up around who said what, when, to who and how. Bitter words and hurt feelings can result from arguments about the visible effects, rather than the deeper causes of strife between a couple.

Divorces and separations are often seen to be based on a couple's poor style of communication, a short attention span or a failure to listen to the other fully.

The truth of the matter usually lies in none of these effects. The cause is usually something like this:

* an inability to manage the needs of a me me ego

* not being conscious enough to manage strong feelings in an adult manner

* not putting the interests of the relationship (which is different from either individual) before one's own

The fact of the matter is that most of us are not yet grown up enough to serve the other in a relationship. We can do it when we are feeling happy, relaxed, pleased with ourselves and our lives. But when we most need to do it: when we are angry, frightened or irritated, we don't love enough to put our ego needs to one side. At these times what we most love is getting our own way, having our view properly heard and considered, getting an apology or telling the other person how they should be.

When we are like this we aren't fit for relationship. We can only serve our own interests and egos. Most people grossly underestimate the amount and the quality of love required to grow a relationship. This type of love serves truth and truth has nothing to do with who said what to whom and why: these are incidentals and minor skirmishes. They are the effects of the cause which lack of love produces.

The truth of love in a relationship is whether or not you have enough of it to put your idea of how the other should be to one side long enough to see what it is you are loving.

It is perfectly possible for one person to love another, but not to love enough to be willing to see the truth of what they are, without wanting to change that to suit themselves. If you don't love the other more than your own need for things to be a certain way, why be in the relationship?

This is not to say that we are all perfect and that there is no need for growth and change within a partnership. A relationship is the perfect mirror to show us our mistakes and places where we can refine the Grace of what we are.   But the ways of growth employed by love and truth are nothing to do with fighting, shouting, screaming and rowing. These are the 'I want' ways of the ego and the tantrums of spoilt children.

So choose your 'battles' carefully. Ask yourself what your desire to change the other is really about. Make sure it wouldn't be better to change yourself instead

Notes:

117. Why not inhabit your body

We take for granted that we will live safely inside our bodies in this life, but that isn't always the case. When we are stressed, over excited, ill, upset, shocked or in pain, some of us 'leave' our bodies to fend for themselves and go walkabout.

How does this happen? The layers of the energetic field that surrounds us and makes up our subtle bodies, slips upwards, sideways, backwards or forwards. This means that we can be above or otherwise outside ourselves energetically.

Have you ever heard an angry person explain, 'I was completely beside myself,'? This describes the out of body state very well.

For some individuals, this is an almost constant state of affairs and a habit. For others, it describes what happens to them once in a while.

When you are 'out of your body' you will feel spacey, airy, vague, forgetful, not quite in control, physically clumsy, uncoordinated, and find it hard to concentrate. You will neither hear, nor see as well as normally, you might feel sleepy and out of touch with people and life generally.

If you feel this might apply to you, try this grounding exercise once in a while:

* Sit or stand comfortably with bare feet flat on the floor

* Wait until your breathing becomes quiet and steady

* Become as acutely aware as possible of the sensation of the ground contacting the soles of your feet: stay with this feeling until it becomes strong

* Begin to visualise your feet taking root in the ground, rather as if you were a tree

* If you like, imagine your roots pushing down into the earth

* Feel the natural energy of the earth rising like sap up through your roots, your feet, legs, genitals, hips and so on, up through the body, invigorating and enlivening you.

* Imagine a clear white light entering the top of your head and flowing down through your body to meet the earth energy. See the energies mingling and then flushing through you, down your legs and feet and back into the ground.

* Take a few deep breaths, feel the ground contacting the soles of your feet and shake yourself gently.

* Eat a meal with some protein content

* Stop as many times as you think of it through your day and notice the sensation of your feet on the ground.

You will notice a qualitative difference when your physical body is firmly in the middle of your subtle or energetic one. Your powers of concentration, your sense and the ability to have a Graceful and immediate presence in your own life will be increased.

Notes:

118. Know what the West wind smells like

We drive along the motorways, passing vast tracts of land to the right or left without getting a sense of the shape of the land outside the three lanes we are inhabiting.

The train moves us steadily and speedily from south to north, but what is just over the horizon and out of our view?

We shape and size the countryside by the direction and time the road or the railway takes through it. We don't really know where we are.

We look this way and that, but toward which point on the compass are we facing?

The wind tousles our hair, but does it blow from the west or the south?

We are often ignorant of the shape of the land and its north, south, east, west qualities as shown us by the seasons, the wind, the sun, the flora, fauna and physical characteristics.

Wake up! Reclaim knowledge of your own land.

* learn the difference in smell between the south and the west wind

* identify the dryness or the hint of rain to come in the air

* notice the blueness in the morning light and the yellow quality in the afternoon

* leave the motorway at an unfamiliar place and get a different perspective on the shape of the towns or countryside

* notice the first hazy greening of the air around trees in spring. This happens just a few instants before the bud breaks into leaf

* learn to sense which compass point you are facing at any given time

* develop an internal map of the shape of your land and the direction in which you are travelling

Don't let the motorway or the railway line define your idea of how things are geographically. These tend to be linear structures taking the most direct route from somewhere to somewhere else.

Make time to set your own direction. Take the curvy pathways that Grace your way. Claim the land. Know the smell of the west wind.

Notes:

119. Get your boots dirty

A lovely woman I know bought some walking boots and when she walked in them she went round the puddles instead of through them just as if she still had her ordinary shoes on.

How often in our lives do we decide we want to take a less direct route through our difficulties? We do this to avoid meeting the difficulty or the test head on. This is rather like the woman in my story who wanted to avoid getting her boots dirty even though they were designed for that purpose.

*   human beings are 'designed' to be much more resilient than we give ourselves credit for.

*   we have much more strength than we usually call on in difficult times

*   we are much less helpless than we were when we were very young

*   our lives, no matter how difficult, have given us the tools and experience we need to face our future less fearfully and more directly.

It is time to begin to recognise ourselves as resourceful enough to meet our challenges successfully.

There are many opportunities in life where we are presented with some sort of test or difficulty. The choice we have is to tiptoe round these or go through the middle to the other side.

We can take the long way round and the easier option if we want to. But we need to realise that we have all the personal resources and 'equipment' we need to meet life's tests for us head on.

The choice is yours. Do you want to find out whether your boots will keep the water out or not?

Notes:

120. The awfulness of needing to win

We all like to experience the feeling of getting it completely right, being the best at what we do or leading something special once in a while.

But for some people it is necessary to win all the time. Everything they do must produce a better result than the efforts of others. They must always be seen to be top dog in whatever they are involved in.

We might be tempted to think of these people as 'showing off'; doing what they do for the admiration it brings them from others. Of course this does happen (and it brings them animosity and envy too), but being admired by others isn't the deepest motivation for their need to win.

Some high achieving individuals are motivated to be constantly best because they can't cope internally with the feeling of being anything else. Letting their standards slip can result in confusion, pain and huge amounts of self-denigration. Why should this be?

* Bright children are often praised and given extra attention because of their gifts: their ordinary progress goes unnoticed and unremarked.

* Some children are fortunate enough to be good at almost everything: they are completely used to it and never get used to being less than, not as good as, or coming second.

* As gifted young people grow up, they are completely certain of their ability to win, but they are never given the opportunity to learn to lose and still be ok

* High achieving adults find succeeding easy and they naturally avoid those activities where they are not sure they can excel.

The more ordinary mortals amongst us celebrate our successes and usually manage to find a degree of Grace around our failures. In this way we gain balance and equanimity: we don't become addicted to our own success.

The winners amongst us are not so fortunate in many ways. The ease of their winning eventually ceases to bring them the glow of pleasure experienced by the majority when things go very well.

When the awful day comes where their winning ways let them down, they often don't know how to cope, sinking deeply into shame and not understanding why they feel this way. It is hard for them to undo the patterning of childhood that has served them well (apparently) throughout adult life.

The challenge at this time is to begin to see the lack of balance in their lives and to understand that they too are ok when they aren't the winner, the special one or the star.

Let us bring up our young people to understand that we really appreciate it when they do well, but equally we admire them when they maintain their dignity and Grace in times of disappointment and failure. The bribe of our enthusiastic love for their achievements is eventually unhelpful and breeds in the necessity to win everything to maintain that level of approval.

It is in our failures and our mistakes that the strength of our spirit shows through most. I once knew two men who as part of a mountain climbing party didn't quite make the summit. They went back to high camp, one of them not able to face anyone afterwards and the other watching his companions' progress through binoculars, waved them down, greeting and congratulating everyone who had been successful. I knew his pain at not making the summit was huge but larger still was his heart and his generous spirit. At that moment he became my hero and remains so to this day.

Notes:

121. Releasing the energy we use for moaning

Sometimes we have a niggle on our minds, or a grouch or grumble
that begins to take up a lot of our thinking time. We might talk
about it to other people. Perhaps it becomes the first thing we think
about when we open our eyes in the morning, or maybe we lie
awake at night mulling over what we see as wrong or difficult or
intractable.

It really is quite amazing how moaning can take us over. Even the
tone of our voice changes to a whingey, whiney note. We begin to
let our niggle or gripe into every aspect of our lives. If we're lucky
others might tell us to stop moaning. If we're not they might avoid
talking to us.

Usually the content of our moaning is about something we feel we
have no control over, something that is being done to us. We feel
powerless to do anything but moan about it. We think that moaning
in itself, is the only thing we can do to change our circumstances.

Of course, moaning never really changes anything except to lower
our own energy and that of those who have to listen to us. But
what can we do instead?

We can change our thinking mode from problem focus to solution
focus and get our creative juices working instead. How do we do
this?

* A. Describe the current negative experience that is triggering the
moaning in three clear sentences. Sit and look at it to check you
have written it accurately without the embellishments that moaning
sometimes adds to situations.

* B. Next consider the situation in question and describe what
would be happening if it were good, more positive or right for you.
Write this down in three sentences too.

* Then check whether your positive description of the situation is
viable, possible or doable given your resources and skill. If not,

amend it until it becomes achievable, albeit with hard work, courage, time or effort on your part.

* C. Next write down the steps you (not others) could take to move the situation from where it presently is, toward your positive description of how it could be. Make these steps small, incremental movements that will move you from point A to point B.

* Set yourself goals and dates by when you will attempt these steps. Tell someone you trust about your action plan and get them to support you.

You may think that the things that you moan about are nothing to do with you. This is not Truth. Anything that negatively affects your life is to do with you because you are allowing yourself to be affected in this way.

When life appears to throw difficult situations at you over which you appear to have no control, the work is to minimise the affect on your life and to increase your focus on what is good for you.

None of us can predict when something upsetting will disturb us. With practice we can cease our moaning and develop a more solution orientated approach.

We can become completely sick of our own moaning voices: far better to decide what we want instead and to go for it. That way we release large amounts of creative energy and become much nicer to be near.

Notes:

122. You Identify with what!?

When you talk with your friends or when you are introduced to a stranger and you are asked all about yourself, what do you choose to tell them? Out of all the things you could say about your life and your experience, which story do you recount? Why do you always tell some things about yourself when you leave other things unmentioned.

* If you and I were standing together now and I asked you to tell me about you, what would you tell me?

Think about it. What is it you most want me to know about you. Why those things and not the others?

* If you were sitting alone thinking about yourself, would you consider the same facts: the same story?

We all have a life story with which we can come to identify completely. When we want to let people know who we are, or when we are thinking about ourselves, this is the scenario we use to describe and label our lives. Eventually we come to be our story and it patterns our thinking. Rather than keep the story for others, it is what we tell ourselves about our sadnesses, hardships and heartbreaks in our lives. What's in your story?

* reasons why you weren't able to do or achieve something?

* how and why your love relationship didn't work out?

* where all your money went and how you are having trouble managing financially?

* the state of your health and what that prevents you from doing?

Once we have become attached to our own sad story, we begin to project it forward to shape our future:

* being unable to achieve in the past becomes 'I will never be able to achieve anything I want to. I will always fail'.

* having your heart broken by a lover becomes 'No-one will ever love me. I shall always be alone'.

In this way, the story from the past becomes a pattern for our lives to come. Rather than wishing to be rid of our story as you would expect, our attachment to it becomes stronger and stronger. Why should this be?

* It is familiar to us and we feel at home with it despite its negativity.

* Better 'the devil you know'.

* We believe we have proof that it is true for us as we notice the themes in our story cropping up over and over again.

We hold the 'truths' in our story to be self-evident forgetting they are based on our one-dimensional experience. Despite what we believe about the other characters involved with us in our story, we were not the only ones who were hurt or in pain. But we tend to see things from the position of 'I' and begin to enjoy the familiarity of the suffering that causes us. That we were ever alone in the suffering caused by our sad story is an illusion. It is time to let it go and move on.

Moving away from our story can be a frightening thing to do. Our story brings us some certainty in an uncertain world. It tells us clearly how little to expect in terms of money, love, luck, friendship, opportunity. Even though it is telling us not to expect much, we will settle for this rather than take our chance with the unknown.

However, you cannot commit to the scraps your story leads you to believe are your due, without making yourself and your life very small and sad. Why identify with so little.

Let go and grow Gracefully large. Identify with Life, not pain.   Be a person, not a story.

Notes:

123. So you think you want democracy done to you?

When people want to change things, to have more choice, to become more personally empowered, they often look 'out there' for the invitation to act.

A cry is often heard pleading for more democracy in whatever systems they are in: school, business, church or family. The complaint is usually that they don't have enough say, want more freedom, aren't able to insist on the right to do it their way. They say they are looking for democratic solutions to the problem of being told what to do. Then they wait.

What are they waiting for? What do they hope will happen next? Often such people are waiting for someone to tell them that it's ok to do what they want.

This looking outside themselves for permission to change or to do things differently is often a sign of not being ready to do so.

Your share of the power is not bestowed upon you by anyone else. It is already latent within you and requires an internal response, shift or some sort of personal realisation to activate it.

Part of that shift is to take personal responsibility for being a bystander in lives where we feel unable to act in our own interests. We need to take back the blame we have projected upon others for our own inability.

Those that complain of oppression are not yet able, for many reasons, to release their own power to act and make that shift. Why is that?

* Perhaps we are too weakened by our circumstances to do anything other than survive another day. Sadly, for some beings in our world this is the case.

* Perhaps we are too scared to open our mouths and say, 'no more'. We may see that we have become victims but feel too afraid to try to change it.

* Perhaps we have got used to others doing things to us or for us and are too lazy to assert ourselves, preferring to moan and blame them instead.

All these reasons may be true and yet there are attempts being made by ordinary, oppressed, frightened, sick, uneducated and erstwhile lazy people to change things for themselves so that they can share power with others in the world.

What these people have in common is that they take up personal responsibility for releasing their own power to act. They stop waiting to be invited by others to do so and they cease blaming others for what they didn't do in the past.

How long will you wait to be invited to step up, out or forward? If you look outside yourself for permission to move into your power, you could be in for a very long wait.

Notes:

124. The underrated quality of Followership

Men and women have, since earliest times, striven to be leaders. Today, business schools worldwide cram their students with the principles necessary to be top of the tree and to lead others.

Even parents considering their very young, smile with pleasure at the first signs that their child will assert themselves over others to get their own way in the sandpit.

But if all those with leadership aspirations get their way, who will they lead? Who will be left to be followers? If no one is left, or if no one is willing to follow, who will the leaders lead anyway?

Why is it that our egos are so offended by the idea of following the leadership of someone else.

When we are not in pain or in the grip of our egos, most of us are able to accept that some of us are more suited to this, and some more suited to that. When we can accept this fact we also realise that we are not equally endowed with the skill and temperament that fits us for either leadership or followership. There is no natural superior value in either of these two states: both need the other to function. However, most people would choose to lead whether they were ideally fitted for that role or not.

We all have a place in the order of things, but some of us are not able to value ourselves and the place we find ourselves in. This can make us restless and unhappy, lacking the discrimination to find our natural place and to be comfortable there without resenting what others have.

Consider the skills and attributes that are necessary to be good at following or being lead by another:

* Followership requires the strength of purpose to value the role and to serve from that place.

* Followers need to develop the discrimination to choose their leaders well, based on sound principles and transparent criteria.

* Each follower needs to be clear about when to follow an earthly leader and when the call of universal law or spirit is the superior instruction

* Those who follow must be prepared to challenge the leader if necessary but to do so from a balanced and practical place. The idea is to help the next proper leadership step to take place.

* A follower must hold a great deal of power, as no-one can be led without their agreement.

So are you up to the task of being a follower? There is plenty to do and little acknowledgement in modern life for doing it well. Horses are a bit smarter than we are about all this. When a horse running in a group fancies a spell of leadership, it pushes through to the front. Having done so and if it doesn't have a rider urging it on, it takes a look around, appears to lose interest and either falls back or allows another horse to overtake for a while. It then settles down within the body of the group to follow the leader contentedly.

Sometimes what we think we want isn't so attractive at all when we get it. Find your place in the order of things and be grateful for it.

Notes:

125. Are you a hard or a soft centre?

What is there at the centre of yourself that seems to remain always the same? Is it a core of belief or faith?

Or is it a habit or feat that seems to be permanently there no matter what?

What we have at our core has been saved up as surely as a child puts coins into a piggy bank. Little by little we develop a central store and whatever is in it seeps through us to give us our 'flavour' or approach.

We are rather like a box of chocolates: we have a hard or a soft centre.

We can be hard, rigid and defensive inside; used to hiding our hurts and protecting ourselves.

Or we can be soft, flexible and undefended, with faith in ourselves and/or a higher power.

How we perceive ourselves and our lives is instrumental in deciding whether we are hard or soft at centre.

The same circumstances can produce a defended or undefended approach to life. It depends on whether we view those circumstances as ultimately or wholly positive or negative.

Most of our ideas about whether the world is mostly a dangerous or a generally benign place were formed before we could truly discriminate about the level of threat we were being exposed to.

This means that it would be worthwhile as adults to reconsider the dangers that frightened us as children to see whether we still need to defend ourselves against them.

This inquiry work may not prove easy, but with perseverance can bring success as we realise that there is rarely anything worth defending against in the way that we have been.

You too can be a soft centre. Then you will be able to use the energy you've been using to fight off the enemy to welcome in the allies instead.

Notes:

126. Leaning Back and Letting Go

I often look at the trees, so stark and bare of leaves in winter, and wonder whether they worry that they will never be green again.

Do the dried up ponds and the reduced rivers fret that abundant water will ever fill them up again?

I wonder whether the thorny rose bushes of the cold months remember the feeling of bursting into fragrant bud in the summer.

Nature appears to have such a Graceful faith that good times will come again: an acceptance of the process of dying back and springing up. When it is time for plants and trees to give up their petals and leaves, there doesn't appear to be anything other than a leaning back against that knowledge and a letting go.

If only we possessed a Graceful faith such as this we could let go of our problems and hand them over to life, love and Spirit. But instead we become more and more addicted to our struggling, trying and hanging on.

What would it be like if nature did that? No leaf would ever fall, but would become browner and drier on the bough. No petal would ever drop, but would wrinkle, fade and wilt on the stem.

And that is exactly what happens to us. We become less vibrant, drier and crisper, but we never fall back to lean against the Grace that would sustain and refresh us. We go it alone, struggling against inevitabilities and something in us dies while we still live.

Try, or at least consider this:

* Mentally surrender your fears to Grace

* See Grace as the spirit, which sustains all living things: the invisible growful principle that produces leaves on seemingly barren trees in spring

*   Surrender yourself and your difficulties to this principle

*   Lean back against it and know that you won't fall farther than you need to

*   Let go of your idea that struggling is noble

*   Be prepared to wait for your own spring to come

You are no less than anything in nature so why is it so difficult to accept that you will be renewed and refreshed when you need to be. In our cleverness, we have learnt to interfere in perfect processes and value our independence over our faith in principles greater than ourselves.

Lean back and rest. By now you have surely earned it.

Notes:

127. There is Her and Him and there is It too.

Do you know that there are three beings in every couple?

No, I'm not telling you that your partner has another lover. I am suggesting to you that there is you, he/she and the Relationship itself. Most people seem to be completely unaware of this third corner of things and as a result, fail to give their relationship much consideration whatsoever, even though they love each other very much.

This failure of consideration is the major cause of breakdown in the way people are able to love each other. Then the relationship becomes like a child that is never fed, gradually dwindling away.

Think of it this way:

* When two people meet and fall in love, the connecting place for their energies, hopes and fears is in the relationship itself.

*Their love creates something that is neither just one, nor the other, but a separate field of energy that feeds them both – as long as they both nourish it.

* This 'field' is the energetic home of the love that is contributed by the couple. It stays alive and vibrant only as long as it is cared for and considered.

So what would this consideration consist of?

* Consideration would consist of attention by the couple to the **way** they do things, rather than exactly what they do.

* The quality of the attention given to nourishing the relationship is of paramount importance and takes priority over **everything** else the couple do. No job, no house, no friend, no car, no amount of money and even no child is more important.

* The state of the relationship (healthy, unhealthy, growing, shrinking etc) is of the utmost interest to the couple and time is set aside to talk about this every day.

* The view of each person about what needs to be given and taken to and from the relationship is spoken out loud, each to the other.

* A consciousness of whether the relationship wants to continue or is ready to end is developed by each person.

So moving in together, starting to make love or getting married doesn't automatically provide the he, she and it partnership. If the space that should be occupied by the relationship isn't occupied and nurtured, the couple remain as individuals.

This deprives the couple of their foundation and true home. What a tragic form of homelessness this can be.

Notes:

128. The many I's versus Unity

There are many I's inside each of us. One I may be kind and another may be cruel. One I may feel that it is important to tell the truth and another tells lies. One I may decide to get up early and another may oversleep. One I may promise to love only one person for ever and another may not keep the promise that the other I made. One I may realise that money is tight, but another I might go on a spending spree. One I may spend most of its life working to pay off the debts that another I has created.

Why are we so split? Why do so many I's exist inside one person? What can we do about it?

The answers to these and many similarly deep questions about humanity will keep those on a self development path busy for years to come. And the answers will be different depending on which branch of that long path is taken.

However, when the paths have finished diverging and converge again to form the main highway into the mystery, each traveller will probably hope to know more about what the union of all those I's is like and how to achieve it.

But what about now? What is the most useful thing that we can begin to do in the present moment:

* Decide which I is reading this and what that I thinks about what it is reading.

* Notice when a different I starts to butt in and a different perspective shows up.

* Be aware of the shift between one I and the next. Is that shift mostly emotional, intellectual or physical?

* Notice what state heralds in a new I. Did you invite the new I in or did it come unbidden.

* Perhaps each I comes with a different mood or a different mood comes with each I. Which way round is it for you?

* When all of your I's seem to merge, what does that feel like? Does it happen often and what seems to herald in that 'union' in you?

That feeling of union needs to be recognised, and named as often as possible. Our brains develop firm links and pathways around repetitive experiences. Make sure your brain knows more about your unity than your disunity. You can do this by deliberately recreating the experiences of unity in your life and not concentrating on times of disunity. That way your brain will make the linkages that swiftly recognise unity and 'prompt' you into a corresponding emotional state more quickly.

The many I's that help us live and grow are neither good nor bad. The promptings of some will help you to develop and evolve. Others will not. In our still moments it is easy to be clear which are which.

Notes:

129. A low, low day

Sometimes, even before your eyes open, you are aware that you don't want to face this day. Something about it seems wearying or uninviting. You don't feel any enthusiasm for getting up and getting on.

There may be no reason for this that you can think of. You didn't go to bed too late last night. You had no bad dreams. There is nothing particularly unpleasant in your day that you are dreading. You may even have been looking forward to today when you went to bed last night.

Yet the you that went to bed last night was content and happy enough. So what happened to you during sleep that meant everything seems grey and unwelcoming this morning? It's almost as if a 'shadow' of sadness or lowness has settled on you during the night and you can't get rid of it.

Sometimes we just have to go with the way things are. We can become as active as possible (although sometimes this is difficult when we are feeling low), in the hope that the exercise will shift the mood. Often though, this just doesn't work.

It may be best to go with the flow of things without trying to force ourselves into a different mood or space.

* Do what is absolutely essential to do and leave non-essentials for tomorrow

* Make no major decisions, purchases or agreements until you feel better

* Eat light, easy to prepare meals and drinks

* Tidy the room you are going to spend time in, but leave other housework for later

* If you are at work, do most important tasks first

* Don't blame yourself for how you are feeling and remember it will pass

We have a softer, hazier focus at times of physical and emotional lowness, and often we can't concentrate for long periods of time. Do the things that are best suited to your present state.

Beating ourselves up because of our lowness is a bit like a bad tempered drayman, beating a tired horse to pull a heavy cart up a steep hill. In the end, everything grinds to a halt.

Who knows why our body, heart and mind sometimes refuse to be driven in the usual way. We have to trust that this is for a reason and that tomorrow will be a better day. In the meantime be as still as your life allows and be Graceful in the space you find yourself in.

Notes:

130. A high, high day

Sometimes we could just take off like a rocket and travel up, up, up.
Our excitement seems connected to our core somehow and
everything feels so wonderfully loud and celebratory.

Often these feelings are shared with others and then the effect is
multiplied as we jointly realise our euphoria in unison.

At other times, the celebration is personal: something we hoped for
has happened, something we feared would never be ours falls into
our lap.

The euphoric feelings ripple out from our core and everything seems
more beautiful, more full of potential and promise. All our fears
seem groundless and just for a while it seems as if we could achieve
anything we put our minds to. What a seductive feeling that is.
Physically we feel well. Our faces and bodies reflected in the mirror
appear beautiful and pleasing to us. We look slimmer, younger and
altogether more vibrant.

If only it could last.

But it doesn't and couldn't because it isn't real. It isn't any more real
than our low feelings and our misery and feelings of isolation. We
create our euphoria just as we create our misery: both are either
end of the same phenomena.

Does this mean then that we shouldn't feel either? It is probably
better if we can witness these swings of feeling rather than
becoming lost in them. Riding on such a see-saw can almost be fun,
as long as we don't mistake the see-saw for real life and find
ourselves unable to get off when we want to.

* Observe your feelings fully. Use them to tell you what is really
going on in you and your life

* Don't distance yourself from your feelings in order not to feel:
engage completely but don't become 'just that'.

* Watch the highs and lows of your life from a deeply peaceful central place. Be aware of the transitoriness of your euphoria and your misery. Ask yourself 'what is this for?'.

* Notice how lows follow highs as surely as night follows day

* Teach your mind to centre and calm itself. Use your emotions to help you create positive and repetitive patterns of equanimity

What sort of life is it that you and your emotions are co-creating? It is vital that you pay attention to this, as you have to live in your own creation.   If you want to live on a seesaw that is up to you, but it will make you very, very tired and you may forget how to get off.

Notes:

131. What do you do with your 'waste'?

Do you ever take your rubbish to the dump? Do you put your paper, plastic and tin into recycling containers? Do your food and vegetable scraps fester in a smelly container until they become compost? Are you relieved to have somewhere to get rid of all that stinky or unwanted waste? I'll bet you don't hang around the dump too long either do you? It's not the place to stop for a chat with friends.

If only it were so easy to get rid of the wasted days, aborted attempts to do something, broken love affairs, useless ideas, failed hopes and poor decisions. Each of us lives a life that is full of such waste.

For those of us that develop our night time dream lives, most of this detritus is dealt with there in a specialised and effective psychological process. For others the weight of the waste of our lives presses down on us and affects the way we feel about ourselves in a negative way.

Regrets, self-dislike and a disgust at our own wasteful practices in life often occupy us in therapy, or in complaining to our friends and family. Others of us lie awake at night going over and over the things we have done with our time that have turned out to become a waste of time.

This lying awake and pondering on negativity may seem to be more of the same: more time wasted on useless thinking and regret, or it may be the best process human beings have for disposing of their personal rubbish.

Night is an excellent time for dealing with our wasted stuff because it is so private and we can display our shame without interruption. (Haven't you ever wished you could visit the dump at night and throw away all those household items that you should probably sell or take to the charity shop, but just want to be rid of now?)

Cultivate some new ideas about the use of lying awake at night, thinking about your 'personal rubbish':

* Think of the quality of night: dark, soft, scary, lonely.

* Let the regrets and the recriminations come: when you can't sleep, use the time to get rid of every vestige of your unsuccessful past.

* Don't worry if your regrets go round and round: that will eventually stop and you will be free of them

* You aren't a bad person if you wish to stop regretting some of the things you shouldn't have done. No-one should do penance for ever and it changes nothing for the better. In the end, penance becomes just one more example of personal waste.

* Check out some of your dreams. Has some of your pain and self-recrimination been taken to your internal dump and gone down the chute for ever?

Allow the darkness of night to bless you and your mistakes. You can use the humility that comes from this cleansing process to set you on a new track without carrying your waste around with you day after day for the rest of your life. You may feel weary after a few nights lying awake, but it's a small price to pay for a cleansing peace and renewal.

And if those considerations still aren't enough to persuade you, try imagining the stink if you don't!

Notes:

132. Compromise and all that

We hear a lot these days about not compromising or being non-compromising in our attitudes to life and to others.

What does this really mean?

* that we should never give way but hold firm to what we have decided to do or be?

* that we should figure out what we want and accept nothing less?

* that we should only spend time with people whose ideals match up to our own?

* that only the best, and nothing less will do?

Is that really what we could or should be doing? How does that work out in practical terms in our daily lives?

* we only do those things that further our own philosophies and goals?

* we never forgive those who we believe have compromised our relationship in some way?

* our hopes are paramount and everything we do should bring us closer to achieving our desires. Anything that crosses us should be sidestepped or not engaged with?

* we decide how our lives should be and only those intentions that bring us nearer to what we want should be given time and attention?

* when a relationship doesn't seem to be running on a parallel track to ours, we should end it?

There are people who run their lives in this way: non-compromising, non-deviating and almost nonhuman. A machine runs along the path set for it until it wears out and stops. Human beings were given the option of changing their minds, not being quite sure or compromising from time to time when they see fit.

Being non-compromising isn't the same as creating our own lives. Creation is an organic process in which there is room for changes of emphasis and direction as it becomes apparent that they are necessary for the evolution of whatever is coming to birth.

There is a time for not compromising, but not all the time. The non-compromising take on life might be valued in today's society, but let us not fool ourselves: there is often a fear of failure behind the rigidness of a refusal to compromise and more than a smattering of me me-ness too.

Notes:

133. Writing into a vacuum

Who is it I write to when I sit here writing? Do I imagine one particular reader, or many different readers? Why am I really writing all this?

When we speak, who do we speak for or to? Or do we speak just to get the words out, and away from us: out of our heads and into the air or onto the paper?

Is speaking or writing the same process when there is no-one to hear: no reader or audience? From where I'm sitting, it feels like half a process. How does it feel to you?

When I read something written by someone else, that feels like half a process too. The disembodied view presented on the paper has become detached from its author. How can a view of mine travel around without me in that way?

When we speak to someone and they listen to what we have said, they may take the memory of our words away with them. Perhaps they begin to agree or disagree with what we have told them. They may add their own views and opinions and then our original message to them becomes changed: firstly by their interpretation of what our words meant and then by what they thought about them.

Once we have spoken or written, our message goes out on its own and ricochets out of our control and assumes a life of its own, quite independent of us.

This loss of control over the effects of our communications out there in the world is similar to the process where our actions, once committed, may have causes and effects unimaginable to us at the time we carried them out.

Do we believe this?

* we are potent beyond belief

* what we do and say will always have an effect

* we may never know or see what effect we are having out there

* it isn't possible for us to do or be nothing

Perhaps the best we can do then is to be sure that we intend to do good before we do or say anything.

Before you communicate in thought, word or deed, be sure that what you are about to do or say is more beneficial to humankind than silence.

Well was it......

Notes:

134. A late frost

About this time of year in England those of us who love to garden are often tempted to plant out our little summer plants and get the flowerbeds in order and the hanging baskets filled and put up.

What prompts this is usually the beautiful late spring/early summer weather and the trays of bedding plants in the shops and garden centres. Unfortunately, sometimes we can rush to get this pleasurable gardening job done a little too soon. An overnight frost can occur almost without warning and kill the tender plants we have gently placed in the ground.

Although we know that this can happen, we still take the chance. We just can't wait for the garden to be blooming again. We also know that summer bedding plants are not hardy enough to withstand the frost, but we have some sort of faith that all will be well. Often it isn't.

The garden isn't the only thing to be touched by a late frost. Often in life our best laid plans fall down because we won't be patient. After all our hard work we rush the last steps and ruin all our work. Is this so for you?

* Do you put the furniture back too soon in a newly painted room, smudging the wall and staining the sofa?

* Do you keep a secret treat secret for just so long, but blurt it out before the due date?

* Do you rush into a new relationship before you have finished the process of grieving for the last one?

* Do you leave your new job just before you would have grown to love it?

* Do you wash the facemask off before the 20 minutes is up because you want to see how your skin looks?

* Do you end your partnerships when you fall out of love and before you begin to love truly?

Why won't we wait? Why are we so impatient? What is the tension that needs to be broken by doing something too soon? Why is quickness so admired and slowness not at all?

There is something for you in the last minutes/hours/days/months before you can explode into action. There is a great teaching imbedded in that pause between the desire to act and acting. Find out what it is for you. Be measured, not previous in your approaches to the important things in your life.

Notes:

135. Dealing yourself a bad hand

Sometimes it seems as if life has dealt us a very poor hand doesn't it. We do our best to struggle through, but we would love someone to deal us a better one.

Luckily help is at hand because today is the day we are going to get some aces. How do I know that? Because I know that however it seems, what we get in our hand is dealt by ourselves. WE are the great dealer in the sky.

Human beings are marvellous creatures with incredible minds. Those minds can imagine, envisage and describe things that are and also things that aren't yet. This faculty was not just given to us for our amusement, it gave us the ability to co-create our lives. Our imaginings are not just about dreams, they have the power to turn fantasy (or what has not yet become real), into fact.

The substance of a thought of an apple pie and the substance of an apple pie out there is surprisingly similar. Each is made up of energy matter: the same waves and particles create each. The thought might well be said to be the precursor of the pie.

The substance of a thought about everything going wrong and the substance of everything going wrong in your life today is also surprisingly similar. One is the precursor of the other.

Perhaps it makes sense to pay more attention to what we think about and imagine. It might be a good time to start concentrating on what you want, rather than what you don't.

Do you do this:

* Wake up feeling heavy, with bad feelings about how your day is going to be?

* Worry about a conversation with your boss and decide he/she will not give you the raise in pay you hope for?

* Decide in advance of a situation that it won't turn out well and that it will all end in tears – yours?

* Choose something less than you really want because you don't want to be disappointed by going for something better and not getting it?

If these sorts of worries and thoughts are the precursor of the realities that appear in your life, perhaps you can now see why.

It is a waste of time to rail at fate for dealing you what you get in your life if you are mentally programming in negativity. Take the trouble to decide what you want to manifest and think about that instead.

The power of your mind is amazing. Try it: deal yourself a better hand.

Notes:

136. The D word

What do you think it will be like to die? Perhaps you have bad dreams about it or maybe you prefer not to think about it at all. But take a few moments now:

* What do you think it will be like to die? Meditate for 10 minutes on that now.

* If you never think about it, why do you think that is?

* What are your experiences of being with someone who is dying? What was easy? What was difficult?

* If you have stood by the dead body of a loved one, what did you notice about it? What did you notice about you?

If you have given good consideration to the above questions, now you **will** be thinking about dying. So what do you think it will be like to experience death first hand?

Perhaps you consider yourself as elderly, but if not, almost all of us know someone who is and who is likely to die in the next few years. How would you describe their attitude to death? Could you ask them about it? If your answer is no, is it your discomfort that prevents you?

Why do we frighten our children with our avoidance of having sensible conversations about death?   We imagine that they won't be able to deal with it or that they would become terrified of the possibility of the unknown. If we are able to balance what we tell them about the rhythms of life that occur constantly, they will learn from an early age about the coming and going of things without undue fear.

Why is it that we deal so inadequately with something that is so inevitable? How are you preparing for the end of your life? Dying is the greatest letting go exercise we get to do (as far as we can know). Can you imagine any other major adventure that you will undertake that you feel so unexcited about and are so unprepared for?

We rarely use the fact that we will die one day as part of our criteria for choosing how we will live. Most of us operate as if there is a tomorrow, another tomorrow, another tomorrow and on and on 'for ever'. This means that some things that we know are important and we put off until tomorrow, will never be done because death will interrupt the tomorrowness of things.

We buy things, collect things and clutter up our minds and our homes with things. We quite forget to buy only those things that will manage without us, because we might not be there one day soon. Someone else will have to dispose of the detritus of our lives. What an act of buck passing that is. Why do we persist with it?

If you lived with death as if it was a wise friend who may come calling any time, how would you live today differently and with more Grace? Think about it and make a few changes. Both life and death are precious. Be prepared to do each equally well.

Notes:

137. I will not – no, I will not...

Sometimes the things I haven't got, don't know or think I can't do close around me like a trap.

I stay inside, forgetting others in my fear and bewilderment.

I become preoccupied and concentrate on the nothingness of the fog that surrounds me.

The electrical wire connections in my head that sometimes work so well become loose and disconnect: flapping around in my brain trying to find something else to connect to.

This flapping and losing and fogging create some sort of juice: a soup made up of memories of past failures and sadnesses.

I marinade in this juice until getting out of bed is almost too much for me. I do this until I bottom out into asking for help. It always comes, but is unlikely to be in a form I immediately recognise until afterwards. The imperceptible lifting of energy and spirits alerts me to the fact that something is turning in me.

The edges of the awareness of that turning are like a lifebelt tossed to a drowner. I can grab it or let it bob by.

I believe I always grab it, but is this true? How many lifebelts have passed on the current without me making an attempt to refloat myself?

* Why do I wait so long before asking for help?

* Is it because from my low state I have no trust in my own recovery process?

* Who or what is it that I need to trust?

It seems that there is a right time, a right lifebelt, a right rescue attempt for each of us. It always has the same quality of appropriateness, timeliness and ease.

The Creator of my understanding (whoever or whatever that is for each of us) is never wasteful.

The upturn in our lives, our hopes and the corners of our mouths always comes.

The trick is remembering that from the depth of our drowning.

Notes:

138. What sort of people would you like your friends to be?

How do you decide whether an acquaintance, or someone you've met is going to be a friend? Is it your decision? Is it theirs? What is the process for deepening the relationship with another human being until you can call them friend?

What do you need to know about them to commit to friendship? Is it based on a physical attraction, apparent similarity of view or interest or geographical proximity (the person next door)? Do you need to admire them, their lifestyle, their morals or values?

Are you the type of person that becomes enchanted quickly, apparently seeing everything that is good in the other instantly? When this happens, do you let them know you all at once?

Or perhaps you decide more slowly whether someone is 'friend material'. Do you hold back with sharing yourself until you are sure?

* Become aware of the growth of the desire for friendship in you. How is that growth triggered?

* What must another person exhibit before you will trust them with your friendship: the right clothes, a love of Spirit, similar tastes in music etc.?

* Do you like people who have skills or attributes that you feel you lack? Is your friendship built on a desire to spend time with what you are not, or are not yet?

What is the 'contract' spoken, or more usually unspoken, that you believe you have with your friends? Most of us don't realise that we have such a contract until the other person breaks or contravenes it.

When this happens we often feel let down, angry and upset that the other can behave in this way. We assume that we had an agreement that our friend would act towards us or others in a way that lined up with our assumptions about them.

Often these assumptions echo our own personal values and ideas of how life should be lived. Sometimes we believe we spot these values in others and then believe we know how they should behave.

When our friend doesn't behave in accordance with our values (and the values we were sure they also held), we feel badly let down and the friendship often ends.

These endings tend to miss the point of what friendships are truly about. It is when we notice the differences in the way we live our lives that the opportunity to express and extend ourselves to others starts.

If we cannot offer this suspension of judgement and desire to connect to each other, what hope is there that the tribes and nations of the world will be able to find peace together? Rethink your situation with your friend. What right do we have to expect anything more from each other than the willingness to be loved? Go to it – you can do it!

Notes:

139. What's on top and what's underneath?

What's on top for you today. Is it something like this:

* I won't get it all done

* Will he think I look nice?

* I won't let them get away with that

* She is the most beautiful woman I've ever seen and she's interested in me!

* I'm afraid of him

If so, what's working away on top for you is your ego. The ego is busy talking, setting up, arranging, protecting, fearing: babbling away ad infinitum; rarely still and never giving you any peace unless.....

Unless you can stop listening to your endless stream of thoughts you will never be at peace. But hang on a minute, did you think that endless stream of thoughts was you and therefore unstoppable while you are alive?

But who then is the you that listens to all that babble? Who is this you who isn't those thoughts and wants peace.

The listener is you, the one who wants to wake up: the one who sleeps underneath all that babbling rubbish on top. How can you stop the babbler and awaken the one who listens? How can you watch yourself having all those ego thoughts, instead of feeling that you are those thoughts yourself and having no choice about how they affect you?

If this is what you want, you are required to become extremely observant and to be intensely aware of your Self as listener as you tune in and then out of the stream of thoughts going on in your mind. Notice how long you can disassociate your Self with the thought stream: at first this may be difficult, but with perseverance the nature of the listener as separate from what is being listened to, will become clearer.

The nearer you become to diving into the silence beneath your thinking mind, the louder and more insistent the stream of thoughts will become. As the ego mind realises that 'the still and listening Self' is awakening, it tries harder not to give up the control over you that it has had for so long.

Continue to bring yourself back to the peaceful position of simply listening and then tuning out of the thought stream. Eventually, the choice of whether to listen or not will be completely up to you: the awakened one who has been waiting patiently for so long.

The prize for learning how to disassociate with the babbling ego mind, is the opportunity to experience your true Self, gently alert, truly alive, still and perfectly at peace. Now that has to be worth all that persevering doesn't it?

Notes:

140. Taking things personally.

What does it mean to take offence? People take offence when someone offends them; says something rude or does something they don't like. What makes us think that it is natural and right to become offended because we believe that someone has behaved in an offensive manner (by our own interpretation) towards us? I would like to suggest that it is as antisocial or offensive to take offence as to give it.

Why should I say this? The problem with taking offence is that it is based on the assumption that the 'injury' inflicted upon us by the other person is personal: an action specifically designed for us and no-one else but us.

Rarely is this true. More often the behaviour springs from the anger, carelessness or thoughtlessness that the other person is experiencing in relation to their own life and nothing to do with ours whatsoever. You might argue that nevertheless they need to be brought to task for their bad behaviour and you might be right, but what makes you think that you are the person to do this?

Choosing to take things personally even when they're not stems from egos over inflated and in charge. It comes from the place of the 'don't you know who I am' stance, and of course, the other person doesn't. They are too busy with their own misfortunes. But they are also coming from the same ego place, although the stance is more likely to be 'I'm not satisfied with my life and I'm going to dump that wherever I can!'.

But what makes it more likely that most of us take offence personally? It is possible that we feel we aren't as good as we try to pretend we are and that the offender has discovered our secret. Many people who frequently feel offended by what others do and say to them have a deep-seated feeling of not being good enough. If we could take more responsibility for these rather raw feelings we have about ourselves, we might not become so angry when it seems as though other people have discovered how 'not good' we believe we are.

Notes:

141. Money isn't it!

Someone I love very much said 'When I was poor I thought that was the reason for all the things that were wrong in my life, but now I have enough money, those things are still there. I guess they were about me all the time, but now I've seen that I can do something about them'.

Money, like anything else in absence, is a distracter, but it is never the core issue – that is all to do with us.

Money is a wonderful energy when there is an ebb and flow; in and out. When it gets stuck somewhere else and we don't have enough, that is inconvenient and worrying. When it gets stuck with us, it's like food just sitting in the fridge and going off – it gets stinky when it isn't used.

It is possible to be very rich and impoverished in other ways. When money, for its own sake is what we worship we grow poor spiritually and lose the plot. Why is this?

Money is a 'means' not a thing of itself. It is a currency, a process, a token, an energy. It is the way modern civilisations have chosen to enable what is known as 'free trade'. Of itself it has no value, but it stands for things that we want or need that do.

When we work we get paid in money. That hasn't always been the case and many things have changed as a result of this exchange. Some peoples' work is judged to be worth more money than others'. We don't often get the chance to put a monetary value on our own work. Other people often decide what our work is worth.

This can mean that we feel that we are worth more or less than others. As we are all equally human, it seems strange that society accepts this system as 'so'. Perhaps the system is kept in place by those whose work has the highest monetary value.

Try revisiting the worth you put upon yourselves and your friends to check that it isn't money or possessions based. Personal value measured in money appears unintelligent as money has no worth of its own. Obviously its value is released when something is done with the money. Sadly, that something is rarely of real and lasting value. This way the money remains just a means without much of an end.

Some people devote their whole lives to creating this 'means to an end'. They seldom seem to be deeply content and happy with the 'end' they buy themselves. Perhaps they believe that if they can just make more and more money, their worlds and they themselves will become perfect.

It is possible that there is nothing that can be bought with money that will create the transformation in ourselves and our lives that we long for.

At our earliest and simplest we were already in our most perfect state. Somehow we retain fragments of the memory of that perfection and long for the beautiful simplicity of it. That longing is usually mistaken as a longing for more of this and that: the things or people that will make us happy if we can afford them.

We need to shed stuff, not buy more if we want to re-experience deep contentment. Treat money with respect for the enabling energy it can be, keep it moving: don't make it the business of your life. Money is for something, it isn't a something in its own right - but you are. You aren't for anything except just being. In deep being you gain true value. So don't **buy - be**.

Notes:

142. Shame and other bogeymen

Generally we have little memory of our earliest days so find it hard to recall the feelings we arrived into the world with or developed very soon after. But as we grow older, we begin to realise that there are some powerful feelings that come to us frequently, perhaps from the past, often without appearing to have a correspondingly significant trigger or source in the present.

For example we might sometimes find ourselves feeling a deep and overwhelming shame that seems to be in response to a small error. We wonder why we are feeling so much in response to so little. It makes no sense.

We might find ourselves suffering deep remorse at having committed the slightest of offences. Although we begin to see that this isn't necessary we don't know why we react in that 'out of proportion' way.

There are a number of theories and ideas of where such unbidden emotional reactions come from and how they they are able to afflict us from past life ideas to the taking on of our parents' pain in utero. And of course, there will be all the earliest experiences of childhood that can seem so traumatic to our infant understanding.

Perhaps the most important thing is to begin to see how we can suffer less shame (or whatever the emotion is for you) when it isn't appropriate to do so.

* The first step is to become aware of shame arising when there is little going on that should prompt that feeling.

* As the shame grows, but before you begin to become distressed by it, remind yourself that, 'this is not mine; I do not have to feel like this'.

* Once you are able to be calm and witness the shame rising rather than being it, tell yourself, 'this is not about now; I do not have to react in this way'.

299

* Return to the situation in hand. Decide how you want to deal with it and move on.

You may have to spend quite a bit of time practicing the first step as it requires a swift response and the ability to deal with what is going on in the outer world and what is going on in your inner world simultaneously.

The ability to witness ourselves in the midst of our rising distress is an everyday example of Grace. We cease to be pulled about by our feelings. We become the sensitive, intelligent creatures we were always meant to be.

Living with frequent bouts of disembodied and deep shame denies the beauty and perfection of your existence.

Notes:

143. Look Out! There goes another one!

As I sit on my veranda clutching a cup of my favourite mocha brew, I am lost in pleasant thought. I am thinking forwards to next Friday when I will be travelling to Pembrokeshire to spend a few days with my dear friends Aileen and Martin. I am imagining long walks, conversations about spiritual matters, shared meals and laughter with my companions. Lovely.

In the meantime, skin has formed on top of my creamy mocha, (I hate skin), the postman has delivered letters, the washing machine has finished its cycle, some of my morning writing time has passed, clouds have covered the sun, a spider's web has appeared on the begonia that wasn't there before and I have lost myself in the future.

It is likely, Universe willing, that the time and activities with Aileen and Martin that I was daydreaming about will happen. Or they won't. But either way, that is all in the future. None of it is real **now!** All the things that are real now and now and now have just passed by unnoticed by me because I wasn't there. Where was I? Somewhere in the future, daydreaming. Body here, mind gone ahead. Lights on, no-one at home. A virtual life.

I go out into the hall to collect the post. I open a bank statement and notice that my lack of new contracts at present means that finances are finely balanced to say the least. I remember this time last year when work was more abundant and the holiday in the Canaries I took to give myself a well-earned rest.

I recall the part of the beach I loved, far away from the hotel, where seclusion meant that swimsuits weren't necessary. The sun and the sea on skin echoed the innocence and wellness of childhood. A glass of rough red wine and a grilled fresh fish for lunch completed the sensory memories of that time, now long ago.

In the meantime, I have missed the weather forecast, the next lot of washing isn't in the machine, the seagull chicks have been fed without me watching and still nothing from this day, this minute,

now, has made any impression on my consciousness.

I have the photos of my holiday and when I am solvent again, I will probably take another well-earned rest. But none of that is anything to do with my life today. So far today, I haven't been present in my life at all. My self in my life in the present moment is virtually absent. Body here, mind gone backwards. Lights on, no-one at home. A virtual life.

I might as well just be a computer programme.

Unless I can agree to be here now, existence is wasted on me. If I were in a coma with my memories and daydreams piped into me electronically, life wouldn't be so different from the way it's been this morning.

Good heavens Jan. Wake up and smell the roses! Or write a Gracenote: that should do it!!

Notes:

144. Why do people make things mean things?

Living is full of days and nights. Days and nights are full of experiences, conversations, people, things and moments. If our living is very full, we often spend our moments giving meaning to the experiences that happened last. In this manner our present moments are full of the meanings we give to what has just happened.

Where do these meanings come from?

How do we decide which meanings to give to our experiences, our days, our belongings, our relationships? Perhaps the meanings we apportion to things are meanings that reflect how we would like to think about ourselves, our lives, our experiences?

And why do people make things mean things anyway?

Things of themselves have no inherent meaning. Our experiences of themselves have no inherent meaning. The adding of meaning to our memory of experiences or our perception of things seems to be our way of giving importance or significance to them.

But why do we have to make our experiences or things important or significant? Are they not just enough in themselves? They just **are**, aren't they?

We just **are**, aren't we?

Oh no, sadly we do not seem able to accept ourselves as we 'just are'. We are not content just to be the way we find ourselves.

Test it out for yourself. When you awake from sleep, experience the just finding of yourself, in this body, in this life. Do not make that mean anything. Do not give meaning to anything you find in or about yourself: just find it.

Do not label anything you find in or about yourself. Don't start up the dialogue: 'I am sad', 'I am well', 'oh no, I have to go to the dentist today'. Do not make anything you find mean anything.

As you subscribe meaning to what you find, you are searching for significance and importance that you can attach to your living life. In worldly terms a life without significance and importance must be full of despair. Significance and importance according to Who? I give my life value according to who or what? To me? That is not Truth.

You do not need to make your life and yourself significant or important. No meaning that you can give yourself, your nights, your days, your relationships, your conversations, your work, your things, your anything means anything. Your persistent search for meaning is born of a desperation to avoid insignificance and unimportance because you believe these are negative states.

You have been listening for too long to the critical voice of your ego which is never satisfied and comparing yourself to what you believe you see of others - and this is illusion.

If you had not, you would know that you don't need a label or a meaning. In your raw, unlabelled, unclassified self without attached importance and the significance of world given meaning or role, you are pure, unpolluted intelligence: knowing all and knowing nothing in the same skin.

So what does it mean? I don't know and I like it that way.

Notes:

145. I really choose my choices?

I was busily thinking about the 'turning points'; 'the cross-roads' of my life. I wanted to see whether there was clear guidance or direction at those times and how I made the decisions I did.

Initially, I could find little direct action or decision that had brought about those major changes in my life.

I realised that I am a very different creature from the one that started on the journey, but that I had no understanding of the pattern of choice and change that my life had taken.

Rather than higher purpose or finer feeling or courageous leaping, necessity or expediency seemed to provide the impetus for major change in my life. But is that really so? Often the processes leading up to the changes themselves appeared incremental and easily overlooked: small steps or movements that over time brought me from where I started to where I now am. Has it really been that haphazard? Is it possible that I have been so totally at the mercy of the wind and the weather? There must be more to it than that!

Then I noticed that after a series of small changes, something larger, more visible occurred. This pattern reminds me of stairs in a tall building: ten steps and then a landing, another ten steps and then a landing - each landing bringing me noticeably higher. On each landing might be different doors that I can go through, or perhaps a window where I can get a new sense of where my climb had brought me in relation to the world outside.

I see now that most of the small steps or stairs have been prompted by necessity. I took them because I thought I had to, and perhaps I did. But that traversing the landings, peeping or going through doors and reorienting myself by looking through the windows to see where I was in relation to the world, was quite a different order of choice. There was a catching of breath after the slow and steady climb, a viewing of the choices afforded me by my changing inner landscape and then a checking out of how to reintegrate the change in relation to my outer world.

What a relief to find some logic and hope in what has seemed so haphazard. I understand my own process of growth and change better as a result of this insight.

Now what about you? What does your pattern of change remind you of: a building, a mountain, a mine, an earthquake, an ocean, an elevator?

Acknowledge your own process and progress of life change. Ask what you can do to get out of the way of your own growth pattern and rejoice in the intelligence that propels you onwards, even when you don't notice the movement.

Notes:

146. Do you have a soft centre or a self centre?

Most of us accept that during our lives we will be dealt, or deal ourselves a few tricky hands. Sometimes life can feel difficult and our deepest hopes and desires are not fulfilled. The human spirit is, for the most part, resilient and we usually courageously go on, knowing that the pain will subside in time.

Often this time of recuperation or recovery will find us quite withdrawn into ourselves. Up to a point this is a sensible strategy, giving us the peace we need to gain insights and lessons from what has happened in our lives.

But sometimes we overdo this indwelling and become completely preoccupied with our lot and the reasons why this or that happened and how to do things better or differently next time.

Our attention is turned away from the world and focussed on ourselves and the minutiae of our needs in a time of grieving and recovery.

Is this the best way forward? It is all a question of degree.

Putting ourselves at our sad centre over lengthy periods of time becomes unhelpful, unhealthy and eventually selfish. We make our problems too big, too overwhelming, too time consuming. We lose the balance we gain from gazing out there, at other peoples' lives and seeing the commonality in our problems.

Introspection can cease to be useful and become a lazy, hazy way of passing time. We get what we focus on and if we focus on our miserable selves constantly, then that is what we will continually get. Continual, self-centred preoccupation is energy sapping and the resulting sleepiness makes it less likely that we can rouse sufficiently to notice what is going on around us.

This rousing and noticing is a balancing activity. It is not intended to take away the pain: life will do that eventually over time. Arousal brings a little more energy, a little more interest, a little more willingness to take part. The body temperature rises, the pulse quickens, the heartbeat increases, the vision sharpens, the sense of hearing becomes more acute as we agree to inhabit our physical bodies and shift our focus from inside to out there.

We might notice what has been going on in our 'absence'. The sun has come out, it has started to rain, the leaves are falling off the trees. We might become aware that others are suffering, or are happy or are speaking to us.

As we loosen our interest in our particular situation, it lets go of us for a moment. We distract ourselves, rather as a crying child is distracted with a toy and forgets why it was crying for a while.

Those of us that are parents will know the benefits of distracting a child away from difficult behaviour over punishing it.

The same technique can be applied to you, unless of course you are addicted to punishing yourself!

Get up, get out there and distract yourself for a while. You can go back to your misery any time you choose, but you may not want to.

Notes:

147. Our ingenuity is limited only by our security

Do you ever feel as if you have been wrapped in cotton wool? Does the vibrancy of your days seem smooth and soft? Do you sometimes long for something rawer, sharper, less comfortable?

We spend lots of time improving our circumstances in whatever way we can. We try to ensure that we have at least the basic essentials of living: enough to eat, warmth, companionship etc. When we have struggled and accumulated some safety, security and friendship for ourselves, we may pause and be grateful. Then what happens?

Some of us begin to miss something, regret something, feel sleepy, stop being creative around our living arrangements, freewheel and lose our impetus.

What is going on? We may have worked hard and our hard won security has been a long time coming.

There are two ways of looking at this phenomenon. The first is that we have become addicted to struggling and trying and suffer withdrawal symptoms from the cut and thrust of the climb to the safer platform we have created.

The second is that for human beings, striving and thriving go hand in hand: our ingenuity and intelligence are called forth when there is something important or difficult to be achieved.

So what are we to do? How do we decide which is the case for us?

As usual, there is something worthwhile in the middle ground to dwell upon. It is nonsensical to rush from one 'battle' to another in order to avoid something else: usually yourself.

It is unwise to sit around too long, enveloped in ease and comfort; becoming bored and therefore boring.

Attempt always to have a place, a time, a situation, a relationship in your life where you don't feel completely secure, where you don't know quite what will happen next, where you don't know all there is to know and where you are not entirely at ease. Always have a small mysterious corner in your existence where you need to employ your ingenuity to make your way through uncharted territories.

That way the adventurer, the explorer, the magician in you stays alive and well. The inquirer remembers how much he or she doesn't yet know and finds reason to keep living each day as if it were the last: with a little fear and a lot ingenuity.

Notes:

148. What to do about the state of things these days?

Sometimes we can feel almost completely helpless in the face of some of the cruelty that man and woman visit upon each other. Perhaps it seems to you that acts of brutality, war and starvation of the innocent and vulnerable are increasing day by day, year on year?

Obviously methods of hurting each other and the weapons available to do this grow increasingly more efficient and terrible in their affect. However, man's tendency to be cruel to man is an old story and not a new one.

Perhaps the main difference is that modern technology assures that bad news reaches us quickly from all corners of the globe. Once upon a time we may never have become aware of strife or trouble that didn't take place within our own village or community.

But the barrage of bad news and graphic images of starving orphans and injured people leaves a deep impact on many of us that becomes hard to ignore. We are touched and changed by it.

The temptation is to accept that generally we can do little and turn to something distracting to take our minds off what we cannot change. Alternatively we may become deeply depressed and feel guilty at our own impotence in the face of so much suffering.

The challenge is not to give into pessimism as this adds power to the negative actions of the perpetrators of violence and cruelty. Instead think of practical actions you can take to enable you to take back the power of rightness that you undoubtedly have.

Take the following steps to consider where you invest energy of one sort or another into organisations, groups, friendships, communities, whose motives don't line up with your own:

1.Make lists of all the organisations/institutions that you have a relationship with; particularly if that relationship involves your money.

2.Do your homework: find out if any of them take part is any practices that deny others their basic human freedoms.   These may be to do with the labour they employ, the governments or regimes with whom they have contracts or where, from whom and on what basis they purchase produce or raw materials. Perhaps it is also important to check from where they raise their finance. (Yes, this will involve you in lots of research, but when you do this you take your place with others in promoting justice for all).

3.Withdraw your patronage and your money from any organisation that doesn't satisfy your scrutiny and find something more transparently ethical.

4.Don't continue to be a member of any social group where there is unkind or unequal hierarchy and importance of each human being within it.

5.Remove yourself from friendships with those who are not just and/or loving in their dealings with all peoples. Remove yourself from those who are prejudiced or use power against others for personal gain.   (Sometimes these individuals may be close to us, so we must do our best to broaden and soften their views before deciding to leave them with a clear conscience). In particular, raise your children to be powerfully peaceful and to use careful and loving discrimination in friendships as they grow. By example is the only way to teach this well. Be peaceful and non violent yourself.

When there is all the above that we can do, why would we be tempted to believe that we can do nothing to end the inequality, violence and cruelty that happens in our world?

Never underestimate the power of the individual to weaken and disempower the seemingly powerful groups that accidentally or deliberately finance tyrannical regimes.

1 by 1 by 1 we can withdraw our finance and emotional support for anything and anyone whose motives and actions are not positively intentioned.

Power and blessing to the 1 by 1 by 1 by 1 people whose numbers are growing daily.   They care and they are making differences. Can't you feel it yet?   Perhaps you are looking the wrong way?

Notes: